Praise fc

Rita has poured her heart and soul into her latest book, *So You Love a Prodigal*, and I'm already thinking of all the people in my life who will benefit from reading it. Not only does she deal with the hard reality surrounding what it truly means to love—and even survive despite loving—a prodigal, but she also provides practical tips for what you should and shouldn't do in the process.

She is careful to qualify that her book is not a guarantee to bring your prodigal (whether it be a child, spouse or other loved one) home, but she does have a wealth of personal experience, has gathered information from others in similar situations and is willing to share her treasure with the rest of us.

~ Jennifer Davis Rash
Editor-elect, The Alabama Baptist newspaper

In Rita Moritz's *So You Love a Prodigal*, readers will find themselves challenged and stretched causing them to identify with the isolation and pain of biblical and twenty-first century stories. In the process, they will learn more about the Heavenly Father who has loved them while they were yet prodigals. The book is easy reading, but not easy feeling—as Rita challenges the status quo society to love, embrace and accept prodigals. Using several biblical narratives, personal stories from her life and the lives of others, poignant poetry and insightful inquiries, Rita guides the reader from loving a prodigal in an unhealthy way to loving a prodigal in the healthy waiting room of life.

I highly recommend *So You Love a Prodigal* to anyone who loves a prodigal, loves someone who loves a prodigal, is a prodigal or once was a prodigal. In its pages, you will find the encouragement, candor and courage to love prodigals and those who love them while loving yourself.

~ Dr. Robert Smith Jr.
Charles T. Carter Baptist Chair of Divinity
Beeson Divinity School, Birmingham, AL

A sure sign of godly character is when we allow our tests to become our testimony for the glory of God. Rita is an example of just this. The godly wisdom that came from her experiences and now comes from her pen in *So You Love a Prodigal* will affect many lives in a positive way and bring much honor to the God she serves. I consider it an honor to pastor a woman like Rita, who has allowed God to turn her trials into triumphs. She is truly a woman of spiritual obedience.

~ Dale Foote, Senior Pastor
Seddon Baptist Church, Pell City, AL

So You Love a Prodigal is that book you read and easily find yourself identifying with many of the characters. Just like the "older brother," we have been self-righteous. Just like the "prodigal son," we have needed the Father's grace. And just like the father, we have all been desperately longing for our loved ones to "come home" with a truly repentant heart. Find your story in this amazing narrative by Rita.

~ Yvette Maher,
Former Senior Vice President,
"Focus on the Family," Colorado Springs, CO
Exec. Pastor, New Life Church, Colorado Springs, CO

I had the honor of serving as Rita Moritz's pastor for a number of years. This allowed me to have a unique, front row seat in watching and helping her through part of her prodigal child journey. In *So You Love a Prodigal,* Rita has modeled II Corinthians 1:4 which says, "Who comforteth us in all our tribulation, that we may be able to comfort them which are in any trouble, by the comfort wherewith we ourselves are comforted of God."

Rita's book offers specific suggestions about what to do and what not to do to help your prodigal and, most importantly, to help yourself. I especially appreciate the emphasis on "self-care" that runs throughout these pages. You will find knowledge for your head and hope for your heart as you digest the words of this book.

~ Steve Reynolds, *Bod4God* and *Get off the Couch*
Senior Pastor, Capital Baptist Church, Annandale, VA

So You Love a PRODIGAL

What You Can't Do, What You Can Do, Why You Can't Quit

RITA AIKEN MORITZ

PRECIOUS PRODIGAL
Precious Prodigal, P.O. Box 125, Cropwell, AL 35054

So You Love a Prodigal
ISBN-13:978-1540460677
ISBN-10:1540460673
Also Available in EBook Format.

Scripture quotations used in this book are from the King James Version (KJV) of the Holy Bible, unless otherwise stated.

Cover Image ©: www.123rf.com/profile_peshkova
Cover design by Elizabeth Little
Book design by Ellen Sallas, The Author's Mentor
www.TheAuthorsMentor.com
Author Website: www.RitaMoritz.com

PUBLISHED IN THE UNITED STATES OF AMERICA

This book is dedicated to all of you
who are walking the hard path
of loving a prodigal
and to the God of Hope,
who will walk every step
of that journey with you.

Table of Contents

FOREWORD
by David Bennett

When I first met Rita, she was in what she called a "temporary situation." Rolling around in a wheelchair faster than I could walk, she and I were seeing eye-to-eye just a few weeks later. Even before she left the chair behind she stood tall in my eyes. Rita reminds me that situations, circumstances, and relationships—including prodigality—are temporary. And though the temporary may last a lifetime on this earth, God redeems all in His time.

So You Love a Prodigal is among Rita's lifeworks. It's not her only work. She continues to reach out to others, see the best, and press on. Hers is a life of service to the Father who forgives and redeems.

You'll connect with Rita's open and honest conversation. You'll feel like she knows you, almost as if she's been where you are. She doesn't sugarcoat anything. She presents the good news that God loves, saves, forgives, and redeems—over and over again.

These pages are filled with biblical truth and stories that will break your heart and then open it to God's healing. But you won't find an instructional manual for fixing prodigals. Instead you'll understand how important it is to take care of yourself along the journey. Most importantly, you'll be confronted with God's gift of joy for you—no matter how much "prodigal" is in you or in someone you love.

Rita declares, "God doesn't make mistakes. His will is going to be accomplished in the lives of your prodigal and mine, whether through their obedience or through their disobedience."

1

Waywardness may appear to be a temporary "condition" or seem like a lifelong career. We're all wayward in need of direction. We're all prodigals in need of a home. We're all sinners in need of a Savior.

Come on home.

David Bennett
Managing Editor
HomeLife Magazine

FOREWORD

by Mrs. Walter S. Beebe

I've known Rita ever since Wally and I led her to Christ many years ago. From the first day, Rita had a heart for others. She consistently shared her faith, encouraged other women and loved the bus kids, those "throwaway" kids no one else wanted.

Wally and I walked through many trials with Rita over the years, and our hearts broke with hers as she tried to live for the Lord during some very hard times. We both tried to encourage her, disciple her and walk beside her through those years. She has remained my faithful and constant friend from the first day until now, and I've watched her grow through her heartbreaks. I remember telling her God would someday use those hard times in a way that would honor Him.

That someday is now with her book, *So You Love a Prodigal.* Rita's book meets the family of a prodigal where they are—in their brokenness—and gives them chapter after chapter of encouragement. Wally and I both loved the beauty of Rita's words, and this book is the perfect example of what we loved about them.

Every page offers a consistent theme of hope and helps the reader to see their circumstances from a different perspective. In her positive, upbeat way, Rita walks the reader through the despair and heartbreak of loving a prodigal and into the confidence that God knows what He's doing.

I'm delighted to provide this foreword for Rita's book because I know her heart as well as her writing. She has an amazing ability to turn a tragedy into a testimony, and she writes from her own experience. I know it will bless many people. If you are someone who loves a prodigal, I know it will be a help to you.

Mrs. Walter S. Beebe
Woodstock, GA

INTRODUCTION

If you have picked up this book, it probably means you have a broken heart over someone you love. While the primary focus of this book is on a prodigal who is a son or daughter, it could be your spouse or someone else who is dear to you, and that loved one has hurt or disappointed you.

When some of my kids first began to act out in destructive ways, my mom was shocked and said, "I would have expected this kind of behavior from almost any of the children in our family except yours." Really? Why would she have thought such a thing?

Because we were active in our church, and the kids were in a Christian school, she may have thought our family was exempt. If that's what she thought, she was wrong and incredibly naïve to think kids from Christian homes don't ever act out.

But don't we sometimes wonder the same thing? If you're like me, you've spent some time asking yourself how and why you have a prodigal. You may have heard your husband's profession of faith or dedicated your child to God when he or she was a baby. Your family may have been and may still be active in church, and all of you may have been leaders in the church, the school and the community. How in the world did it come to this?

Your marriage, which started out full of love and hope, has been destroyed, or the kids in whom you've invested your life have rejected everything you tried to teach them. And you might be saying, "Why me? Why my husband and family? Why my kids?" I've asked those same questions.

Why would I write this book, and why should you read it? Can my book or any book make sense of the wreckage a prodigal has created in your home? Might I have some formula to heal your broken heart and repair the broken relationships in your family?

If that's what you're hoping for, I'm sorry to disappoint you. I don't have any magic words, nor can I promise you your prodigal will repent and return to you, seeking forgiveness and restoration. I wish I could.

I also won't be able to say I know how you feel, although I have my own prodigal. Why? Because even though the experience of joy may be universal, each person suffers the hell of loving a prodigal in his or her own individual way. But you already know that, don't you?

No, I can't do any of those things. However, I have learned some things from the Word of God, from other people who love a prodigal, and from my own journey, and some of those things may help you. Many things are beyond your control and mine, but there are some things we can do to make our situation more tolerable.

Some of those things may also help the people we love, including our prodigal. Most important of all, they may help us to help ourselves. We can make some choices and take some actions that will help us to survive and even thrive in the midst of our pain.

And while I know your heart is broken, I want you to know God uses broken vessels. My own broken heart drove me to the Scriptures searching for answers and hope. In spite of my pain or maybe because of it, I found both.

Rita

PART ONE

Prodigals and Those Who Love Them

"Beloved, think it not strange concerning the fiery trial which is to try you, as though some strange thing happened unto you" (1 Peter 4:12).

If loving a prodigal doesn't qualify as a "fiery trial," I don't know what would. Whether your loved one has been acting out for five days or 25 years, loving a prodigal isn't an easy path to walk. After you've invested your life in your marriage and your kids, you may be asking yourself how this could happen in your family. How could God allow your spouse to leave you or your kids to do terrible things—things that are breaking your heart? Sadly, substance abuse is often part of the problem. When it is, that adds another dimension to the disappointment, hurt, and confusion. Why are these things happening to your family? Why are they happening to you?

Once the initial shock has worn off, the questions become more personal. Who's to blame? Is this because of something I did or didn't do? Am I to blame for what my prodigal has done? While you're examining every detail of your life trying to find the answers and especially trying to figure out who's to blame, your prodigal continues to create chaos in your family.

You wouldn't be the first person who has asked those questions, and you won't be the last. I won't presume to be your teacher because I'm just a pilgrim walking a hard path just like you. However, as we look together at the first prodigals and then examine who's to blame, my prayer is you'll begin to find some answers for yourself.

My Son

For years I prayed to know God's perfect plan
and asked His matchless grace to raise a man.
I watched you grow, and watching, I grew too
and learned from the complexity of you.

So I with love invested through the years
in your young life and that sometimes with tears.
I feared many times the world we knew
would harm, dismay, or bring some pain to you.

I couldn't even guess the things you'd do—
that choices you would make would hurt me too.
Then watching how this world took full control,
I felt it pierce me to my very soul.

I cannot reach you, cannot help or pray
as day by day, you throw your life away.
I know the choice is yours, my son, to make.
But have you realized yet what's at stake?

Your very life may be the price you pay
for all the things, by choice, you threw away.
I want to fight, to rage, to lose control,
to somehow beat this sickness of the soul.

Oh agony of heart—My son! My son!
Who knows the wondrous things you might have done?
But all my hopes and dreams are not for you.
They're worthless things if you don't want them too.

I can't shield you, though I've often tried,
and that would sometimes hurt your manly pride.
But Oh! I loved you, son, and I still do!
And still I pray and hope the best for you.

I cannot help you, son, to leave this hell.
I want to, and I think you know it well.
But only you can find the way back home.
I'm powerless. You must go on alone.

I gave birth to you, and I was glad to give,
but now this life is yours alone to live.
What choices will you make? What will you do
with this rich gift belonging just to you?

Who knows the wondrous things you might do still?
My heart cries out, "Son, if you only will!"
The path you're going to choose demands some thought.
What will you choose—Recovery? Or not?

For this my son was dead,
and is alive again;
he was lost, and is found.
        And they began to be merry.

Luke 15:24

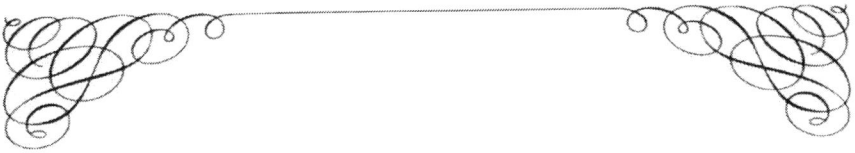

Chapter 1
So You Love a Prodigal

It was more than 20 years ago when I wrote an article for *Educational Leadership,* entitled "Tough Love for Kids at Risk."[1] I wrote that article because I knew America's kids were in trouble. And I didn't need anyone to tell me that because one of those kids was mine.

The statement about kids being in trouble was true then, and it's even truer today. Only it's not just America's kids that are in trouble. Our families are in trouble, our faith is in trouble, and our very way of life is in trouble.

According to the U.S. Census Bureau, just one child in three lives with both parents. Six million children live with grandparents or other relatives, and, for many of those kids, no parent is present at all.[2] Returning veterans come home from deployment as wounded in their spirits as they often are in their bodies, and drug and alcohol abuse have reached epidemic proportions in the United States.

So you love a prodigal. If you do, you're not alone. Although most people don't advertise it when someone in their family is acting out in destructive ways, chances are it's happening. And it's happening in Christian homes like ours.

I've been teaching in Alabama's Court Referral Program for ten years, and I have stopped being surprised when children, spouses, and parents from Christian homes show up in my classes. Prodigals show up in all sorts of families, including those of pastors and other pillars of the community. And I have a prodigal in mine.

Regardless of how you define it, the prodigal has come to mean a loved one who rebels or goes off into sin. He or she is the one who spends resources foolishly or self-indulgently. The prodigal is a foolish, reckless, extravagant person, who has given himself up to what the Bible calls "riotous living" (Luke 15:13). In the simplest of terms, it's those who turn their backs on God and their family's system of values, leaving broken hearts behind them as they try to find "pleasure in sin for a season" (Hebrews 11:25).

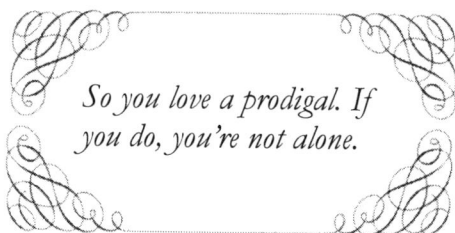

So you love a prodigal. If you do, you're not alone.

Whatever other variables might be in place, all prodigals have one thing in common: they have chosen sin over standards and the world over God and family. Whatever that person's relationship to you, their behavior has broken your heart, shattered your dreams and brought chaos and even shame to you and to your family.

The parable of the prodigal son appears in Luke 15:11-32. However, it isn't the first, nor is it the only example of a prodigal in Scripture. The first prodigals appear in Genesis, as does the first example of forgiveness and restoration.

In Genesis 2:16-17, God told Adam he could eat freely of every tree in the Garden of Eden except for the tree of the knowledge of good and evil. By Genesis 3, both Adam and Eve had eaten of the very tree they were warned about. Immediately, their eyes were opened, they realized what they had done, and they were filled with shame. Then they hid themselves when God came to walk with them in the garden as He always did in the cool of the day.

It's important to remember Adam and Eve didn't eat from the forbidden tree because they were hungry, abused or deprived. They didn't disobey God because He was harsh and cruel or overly indulgent or too busy with His career for them. They didn't make wrong choices, which resulted in such terrible consequences, because of the liberal school they went to, the cold church that "let them down," or the peer pressure of bad friends. Everything they did was an exercise of their own free will.

Let's look at them before their sin and what their consequences were after their sin. As you compare them with your prodigal, you'll see some similarities as well as some results for which you can hope and pray.

They had a godly example: The spouses and parents of prodigals often blame themselves for the mistakes, wrong choices, and even the sins of their loved ones. And the prodigal is more than willing to blame them and to help them to blame themselves. But Adam and Eve couldn't have had a more perfect "parent."

Can you imagine the great God of the universe, the One who spoke the worlds into being, walking with you and having fellowship with you in the cool of the day? Seeing God as He is in all His perfection and glory and being comfortable with walking beside Him in the garden each day? How incredible that must have been!

But it didn't keep Adam and Eve from making the wrong choice and doing the wrong thing. And teaching our system of values by living it in front of our kids doesn't guarantee those kids will make the right choices either.

While we have the responsibility to set a godly example for our kids, our good example alone will not prevent those kids from doing the wrong thing. God doesn't have any grandchildren, only children, and knowing "about" God from your parents is not the same as knowing God personally and having a relationship with Him.

They had a perfect environment: Adam and Eve lacked nothing in the Garden of Eden. God had provided for them in every way. They could help themselves to anything growing in the garden with one exception, their lives had purpose as they did the work God had assigned them, and they had an intimate fellowship with God and the sweet fellowship of their innocent union. How blessed they were. No peer group to lead them astray, no bad examples to follow, no mistakes of others to blame.

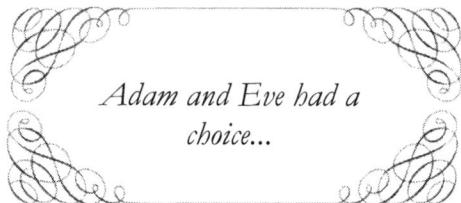

Adam and Eve had a choice...

It's a lucky child who grows up in a home where the Bible is read, where he hears his name spoken in prayer, where church attendance is a family tradition and where, though not perfect, the environment is safe and wholesome. But having those things is not a guarantee the husband or wife will be faithful or the children will live honorable lives or bring joy to their parents.

They had a choice: At any point in time, either Adam or Eve could have chosen to do the right thing. Eve listened to the devil's lies and was deceived into thinking God wasn't being fair. She "saw that the tree was good for food, and that it was pleasant to the eyes, and a tree to be desired to make one wise" (Genesis 3:6), so she took the fruit and ate.

Can't you picture her looking at the tree? I would bet she didn't eat the fruit from the tree the first time she looked at it. However, she was sure standing right next to the forbidden tree when Satan came to tempt her. One tree of all the trees in the garden, and that's where Satan found her. I doubt it was a coincidence.

It's more likely Eve had been thinking about that tree and the fruit on it for a while and had gone back to look at it several times, each time tempting herself to do the wrong thing. She could still have chosen to obey, but she did not.

And what about Adam? I've heard people say Adam chose to sin because of his love for Eve, but I don't believe it. Genesis 3:6 goes on to say she "gave also unto her husband with her; and he did eat." Don't you want to ask why, since Adam was with her, he didn't say anything while Satan was talking to the woman he was supposed to be protecting and leading by example? The simple and more probable truth is he also wanted to eat the fruit and when Eve gave it to him, he accepted it and "he did eat."

Our prodigals made choices too; no one made those choices for them. Nor did your prodigal and mine end up in the "far country" in one giant step. Chances are it was a process where they flirted with disaster, tempting themselves as did Eve. It might be they were deceived, but I don't think they were. People choose to sin because they want to, because they find "pleasure in sin for a season" (Hebrews 11:25).

They tried to cover their sin: The moment Adam and Eve ate of the forbidden fruit, their eyes were opened, and they were filled with shame. They tried to cover their shame and themselves, as if an apron of fig leaves could cover what they had done. And they hid from God.

Can you picture them, fearful and trembling and so filled with shame, they tried to hide themselves from the all-knowing God, who had created them? Most prodigals try to cover their sins as well, in part to avoid the consequences. But I also think shame begins to haunt them early on, and eventually, shame becomes their constant companion, reminding them of what they've done and convincing them there is no hope.

To picture our beloved prodigals, fearful and ashamed, hiding themselves from the people who love them and the God who can redeem them should fill us with compassion. Seeing them this way, the way they really are, should also compel us to pray for them "without ceasing" (1 Thessalonians 5:17).

They blamed others for their sin: Neither Adam nor Eve wanted to take ownership of or to blame themselves for what they had done. Adam wasn't as reluctant now to speak as he was when Satan was tempting Eve. "The woman whom thou gavest to be with me, she gave me of the tree, and I did eat" (Genesis 3:12). It was the woman, God. Yes, she's the one. And if it's not entirely Eve's fault, let me just mention that *You* are the One who gave her to me!

And when God questioned Eve, she responded with, "The serpent beguiled me, and I did eat." She had nothing to say about believing, even for a minute, that God was unfair and was somehow depriving her. Adam blamed Eve, and Eve blamed the serpent.

However, God held each of them individually responsible for the choices they made, although neither of them wanted at first to take ownership of their sin. If your prodigal is blaming you or others instead of himself, it shouldn't surprise you. It's tough to see one's own failings and to "fess up" rather than blaming someone else, whether it's Adam and Eve, the Prodigal of Luke 15, our kids, or you and me. But seeing the problem and owning our part of it are both a necessary part of the process.

They repented and were forgiven: We know Adam and Eve repented and were forgiven because God clothed them in the skins of animals. They had lost their innocence, and they would have consequences. But they also found a time of forgiveness and restoration.

God didn't abandon them because they had sinned and disobeyed Him, nor did God's love for them change because of what they had done. But neither did He shield them from the consequences. His love for our prodigals won't change either, nor will He abandon them or give up on them. Neither can we.

I'm not saying we should get between our prodigals and the natural consequences of their choices, because we absolutely should not. In fact, we need to learn to take a step back and let happen what's going to happen. That's not an easy thing to do when we see our children or other loved ones hurting.

A friend suggested to me when I was going through a difficult period of time that I "just be Mom and let God be God." Wise counsel, but easier said than done. Finding the balance between "just being Mom" and refusing to accept unacceptable behavior continues to be a challenge for me.

It has helped me before, and it still helps me now to remind myself God has a Holy Spirit, who can work in my kids' lives, and that Holy Spirit is not me. My part and yours is to pray and to love our prodigals. God's part is to open their eyes and make the changes.

They continued to serve the Lord: Repentant and restored, Adam and Eve had learned a valuable lesson in faithfulness in the hardest possible way, a way they would never forget. And just as God went looking for Adam and Eve in the Garden of Eden, He will also search out my beloved prodigal and yours.

God won't leave them hiding in sin and shame forever, but will find them wherever they are. Our fervent prayer for our prodigals must be for God to open their eyes and speak to their hearts. It's the only way they will realize what they have done and choose repentance and restoration.

They still faced consequences: Even though they had repented and been forgiven, Adam and Eve still had some consequences for their sin. God didn't shield them from those consequences. And not all those consequences happened immediately.

For Adam, it was the "thorns and thistles" that frustrated his best work efforts from then on, and the "sweat of his brow" didn't make those thorns and thistles go away. He struggled with them for all the rest of his life. For Eve, God said He would "greatly multiply her sorrow," and she would have her children "in sorrow" (Genesis 3:16).

Although Adam and Even died spiritually the moment they chose to disobey God, they didn't die physically for a long time. In fact, their son Abel died before they died themselves. And they are the ones who brought death into the world because death didn't exist before their sin. But after their sin, "death passed on to all men because all had sinned" (Romans 5:12).

What must Eve have thought as she grieved the beloved son she had once held to her breast? Did she finally and fully understood the price her sin and Adam's had cost?

Like our prodigals, neither she nor Adam weighed the cost before making the wrong choice. Sorrow? Oh yes, indeed. And sorrow multiplied. Because when Cain killed Abel, Eve didn't lose just one son. She lost two. But didn't God forgive Adam and Eve? Yes, He did. However, the consequences of their sin had nothing to do with His forgiveness.

Don't misunderstand me. I'm not saying or even suggesting Adam and Eve were responsible for Cain killing Abel. Not at all. Cain and Cain alone was responsible for what he did. But Adam and Eve, who first sinned, passed on their sin-nature to their children.

Although forgiven, they knew sorrow for the remainder of their lives, and their sorrow was both directly and indirectly a consequence of their sin. Our prodigals will face consequences too, and it's neither our responsibility nor our right to shield them from those consequences.

All the components of the wrecked and then restored life of a prodigal are found in the third chapter of Genesis. And although both Adam and Eve tried to "pass the buck" on who was to blame, God held them individually rather than collectively responsible. Neither could they blame the other for their sin.

It wasn't because they didn't have all the advantages. They did. It wasn't because they were deprived. They weren't. And it wasn't because of bad parenting. So who was to blame for their choices? And who's to blame for the choices of our prodigals?

Something to Think About:

Do you see similarities between the behavior of Adam and Eve and the behavior of your prodigal? How are they similar?

Chapter 2
Who's to Blame?

Of course, that's the most important question, isn't it? And looking for the answer to it may be one of the reasons you picked up this book. If you love a prodigal, you've already heard plenty of opinions about why your prodigal is acting out. Because everyone seems to have an opinion, don't they?

You were too strict or too lenient, you gave him or her too much or too little, you were too involved outside the home, or you were too involved with your kids. You didn't take your kids to church, or you forced them to go. You put them in the evil public schools, or you sheltered them too much by putting them in a Christian school, or you homeschooled. Does any of this sound familiar?

Several years ago, I was interviewing parents, teachers, pastors and substance abuse counselors about drug abuse and acting out behavior among teenagers. I asked each one of them that very question, "Who's to blame?" I was astounded at how passionate their responses were and how certain each group was that they had the correct answer. The problem with their assurance is none of the groups agreed.

The parents blamed teachers and schools for not inspiring and supervising the kids. They blamed churches for not reaching out and, of course, the influence of peer pressure.

The teachers cited lack of parental involvement, even implying some of the parents didn't seem to care. The pastors blamed unspiritual parents and ungodly teachers and a general falling away from spiritual things.

Then I interviewed the substance abuse counselors, who were actually working with and helping the kids. Oh, and I need to add these were the only people who were seeing some positive results. Those counselors were the first ones to suggest the kids themselves might be responsible for their choices.

Now wait a minute! Are you suggesting parents don't have a responsibility to their kids? Of course not. Those children God has entrusted to us are a huge responsibility, and God expects us to teach them right from wrong to the very best of our ability. As parents, we need to do what's right ourselves regardless of what anyone else does. We also need to set a good example for our children.

The real question, of course, is more specific. When we're asking who's to blame, the real, underlying question is, "Am I the one to blame?" No guilt is quite as overwhelming as the guilt felt by those of us who love a prodigal. Are they being punished because of something we did, some past sin or mistake? Are we being punished for those things?

Some parents have more tools to bring to the parenting job than others. Regardless of their different levels of parenting skills, most parents love, provide for, teach and try to set a right example for their kids. They do the very best they can with the tools they have. As a parent, I acted in good faith to give my kids every advantage we could afford, to hold them accountable for what they did, and to pray for them and teach them the Scriptures. You have probably done those same things.

You may have sacrificed so your kids could be involved in sports or other activities or worked a second job so they could do those things. You've showed up for PTA meetings, you've taught your kids what's right and wrong, and even set an example to the best of your ability.

Even after everything we parents have tried to do, society blames us when our prodigals begin to act out. It's bad enough when other people say cruel things about how I'm to blame…how you're to blame. Even worse are the things our prodigals blame us for. Worst of all, however, are the things we say to ourselves. Maybe we could consider that perhaps our prodigal, who is 15 or 25 or even 45, might be responsible for his or her own choices?

We do have a responsibility to, for, and about our kids and the things they do and the choices they make as long as they are still in our home and under our control. However, while parents can and must set a good example and should expect and even demand responsible behavior from their kids, there are limits on the things parents can "make" their kids do.

Perhaps the best way to illustrate this is by looking at the lives of two men who were called of God for a specific purpose. We can find valuable truths in the parents they had, the examples and encouragement they had, and how they turned out.

You will almost certainly see some things you have in common with these parents and their sons. Although those two babies started out pretty much the same, the choices they made were as different as day and night. Those two men were Samuel and Samson.

The parents they had: Two women in the Old Testament had similar stories. They were both barren in a time when it was a reproach for a woman not to have a child.

Both of them were godly women, whose heart attitudes were above reproach. And they were both willing to give their sons back to God. In fact, both of them took a Nazarite vow, one on behalf of the child she would bear and the other for both her son and herself for the duration of her pregnancy. One of those women was Hannah.

Hannah, "in bitterness of soul," prayed and wept before the Lord because she was barren (1 Samuel 1:10). As she wept and prayed, she made a vow to God: if He would give her a son, she would give him back to God. He would be a Nazarite, totally dedicated to the Lord. She was in such bitterness of soul as she prayed in the temple that the priest thought she was drunk and rebuked her.

But the Scripture is clear that this godly woman had no reason to be ashamed, and God heard her request and gave her the son she asked Him for. Hannah's happiness must have been bittersweet as she nursed her precious Samuel, knowing she would only have him for three years. After those three short years, she would take him to the temple and entrust him to the care of Eli, the priest. From then on, she would see him just once a year when she went to Jerusalem.

The other woman is not named in the Scriptures, and I'm pretty sure she would be thankful she wasn't. She was the mother of Samson, and her husband was Manoah. The Scriptures don't tell us she wept before the Lord or asked Him to give her a son. However, it's not much of a stretch to believe she did.

How could she not ask God to fill her empty arms, especially in a culture where it was a shame and a disgrace to be barren? She must have been overcome with joy when an angel appeared to her and told her she would have a son who would be a Nazarite from the womb. Can you imagine what delight must have filled her heart, what hope, what rejoicing?

And knowing her son would be the one who would "begin to deliver Israel out of the hands" of the hated Philistines must have thrilled her (Judges 13:5). Her husband Manoah must have been overjoyed as well.

What a happy day it is when you find out the child you have waited for, have longed for, have dreamed about is on the way. And what joy when that day comes, and you have your beautiful, healthy child!

Both Samuel and Samson had parents, who wanted them, who loved them, who cherished them. What a wonderful start to their lives...parents who anticipated their birth with joy and thanksgiving. Now, what about the people who influenced those kids as they were growing up?

The examples they had: When the angel appeared to Manoah's wife and told her she would have a baby, he also cautioned her to not drink any alcohol nor to eat any unclean thing because her baby would be a Nazarite from the womb until the day of his death.

Raising a child is a huge challenge and responsibility in any situation. In the case of this child, it went off the chart. How could she and Manoah know how to raise a child given to them by God for a specific purpose? When she told Manoah what had happened, he immediately went to the Lord in prayer and asked God to send the angel back to "teach us how to bring up the boy who is to be born" (Judges 13:8).

At no time does the Scripture assign any criticism or blame to Manoah and his wife. Godly people, concerned and caring parents, just all around good folks, who did the very best they could to raise a son, one who would love and honor God with his life. I have no doubt they followed the instructions and did their best to train and mold their child into someone who could be used of God.

The three short years Hannah and Elkanah had Samuel with them must have flown by, and I'm sure they poured out all the love they had for him. I'm also sure they trusted Eli to set a good example for Samuel and to teach him about the things of God and about his calling. I mean, they could trust the man of God in the house of God, couldn't they?

However, Eli wasn't even a good father to his own sons, who were "sons of Belial who knew not the Lord" (1 Samuel 2:12). Because Eli allowed his sons to sin when it was in his power to stop them, God eventually brought judgment on both his sons and on him. Because of that, it's hard to believe he was any better an example for Samuel. Nor could Hannah have taught Samuel very much about walking with God during those first three years.

Then the night came when God called Samuel. 1 Samuel 3 tells us Samuel was still a child and didn't yet know the Lord. When God called his name as he lay down to sleep, Samuel thought it was Eli. He ran to see what Eli needed, and Eli sent him back to bed.

It took three times before Eli realized it was God calling Samuel, this child who didn't know the Lord. Since Eli knew the call of God on Samuel's young life, we might expect him to have taught Samuel to be listening for that call. But Eli didn't teach Samuel what to do the way he should have.

The word of the Lord was rare in those days and visions even more rare (1 Samuel 3:1). Knowing that, wouldn't you expect Eli to jump up and instruct Samuel about what he should do? Unfortunately, Eli didn't do that either. Not even close.

Even after Eli realized God was speaking to Samuel, his response was to send Samuel back to bed. But this time he told Samuel what to say if the Lord called him again. I mean we aren't talking about a late night telephone call from Mom.

It wasn't even a telegram from the President. It was the very voice of God calling the child who was in Eli's care.

Where was the excitement? The delight? The instruction? Eli's response showed a lack of reverential awe for the great God he supposedly served. It also showed a lack of respect for the call on Samuel's life and a lack of concern for the responsibility he had to set an example for Samuel.

Two children, loved, prayed for and known to be a gift from God. Samson had the loving parents, who taught by example, rebuked him when necessary and grieved when he did the wrong thing. Samuel had a once yearly visit from his mother. The rest of the time he was in the care of Eli who didn't teach him about the call of God on his life and either couldn't or wouldn't even get out of bed when God spoke to Samuel. If you had to predict how those two boys were going to turn out, what would you say?

I've never met a parent yet who didn't make some mistakes.

The men they became: The first indication we see of Samuel's heart was when Eli told him how to answer if God called him again. Samuel didn't argue or sass. He didn't say how tired he was or how none of his friends had to answer midnight calls. And when God called him yet a fourth time, Samuel's immediate answer was, "Speak; for thy servant heareth" (1 Samuel 3:10).

Here was Samuel, just a child with an absent mom and dad, raised by a wishy-washy priest, one who wouldn't even use the authority he had to control his own wicked sons. Yet Samuel obeyed the first call of God and lived for the Lord all the days of his life (1 Samuel 7:15).

Samson, on the other hand, was a different story. He did so many things wrong, it's not easy to choose just a few. I'm sure his parents saw hints about his nature as he was growing up, but let's start with his choice of a wife from among the hated and ungodly Philistines. When his parents entreated him to instead take a wife from one of the tribes of Israel, Samson planted both feet and insisted on having his way.

On his way to Timnath to marry this ungodly woman, Samson came across the dead body of a lion he had previously killed. As a Nazarite, he wasn't to touch it…it was unclean. However, bees had built a honeycomb in the carcass of the lion, and Samson wanted some of their honey. So he took it. And he not only took some of it, making himself "unclean," but he also took some to his parents making them also "unclean" before the Lord, but without their knowledge. Then he made a mockery of his sin by using it as a riddle.

The list of all the things Samson did wrong would take up a volume by itself. Suffice it to say he was prideful and arrogant, a womanizer and a mocker, who made a joke of his sin. After a lifetime of wrong living, Samson achieved more with his death than he ever did with his life. What a sad testimony from a man who was set apart for the Lord from before he was born!

Two different men, two different backgrounds, two different outcomes, neither of which anyone would have expected. The one thing they had in common was a God who had a plan for their lives. And God's purpose was accomplished in both those lives, one through his obedience and the other through his disobedience.

But what about Proverbs 22:6, which says, "Train up a child in the way he should go: and when he is old, he will not depart from it?" I've seen more parents consumed with guilt and shame over this one verse than any other verse in the

Bible. But their guilt and shame (and ours), are undeserved. We may need to take ownership of many things we have or haven't done, but the path our kids choose isn't one of them.

Have you ever considered this verse might be something other than a promise? Most Bible scholars compare it to Proverbs 3:1-2, which admonishes sons to remember and obey the teachings of their parents because their obedience will bring them peace and long life. And it often does work out that way.

However, I know godly, obedient people who died young or even before they were grown. And so do you. Does that mean God's Word is untrue or unreliable? Not at all. As with the other proverbs, it compares good and evil, wisdom and foolishness, pride and humility and tells us how things "usually" work out.

Whether Proverbs 22:6 is a principle for living or a promise for our lives isn't even the question here. The real question is whether you and I are going to obey God in the rearing of our children. Because I know a couple of things with absolute certainty. One is that I will someday stand before the Lord and answer for whether I taught my kids they were to live for Him.

The other thing I know, and this one *is* a promise, is that God's Word will not return to Him void, but will accomplish what He intends (Isaiah 55:11). Planting the seed of God's Word in the hearts of our children will not only touch their lives today, but it will also bear fruit in the future. You and I have God's promise it will. It might also someday be the path back to the God who loves them with an everlasting love.

Regardless of what we teach them, our kids still have to deal with life and the choices they will make along the way. And just as we didn't always and still don't always choose to do the right thing, neither will our kids. God gave them a free will just as He gave us a free will. As parents, we need to teach our children what's right. Of course we do. And we need to try to reach them for Christ if we can while they are young and their hearts are tender.

But even if we have led our kids to Christ when they were children, their salvation is no guarantee they won't become prodigals and break our hearts. Once we've taught them the best we can, we need to realize the ultimate choices in their lives are theirs and theirs alone to make.

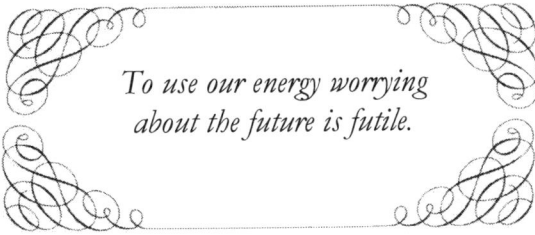

To use our energy worrying about the future is futile.

Have we made mistakes? Of course we have, because we're only human beings. We come to marriage and parenting with no experience; it's *all* "on the job training." And I've never met a parent yet who didn't make some mistakes.

Besides the mistakes all of us will make, we don't all come to marriage and parenting with a well-equipped tool box. We bring our own childhood experiences, hurts, disappointments, expectations and wrong thinking into parenting. I call the sum of those things "spontaneous dysfunction," and every parent I've known, including me, has had to overcome some of those struggles in their parenting.

It could be you got out of bed every morning and said to yourself, "What can I do today to totally mess my kid up and ruin his life?" Of course, you didn't do that. What you did was the very best you could with the skills you had at the time. During a time when my own heart was broken over one of my kids, a pastor friend told me no parents are perfect. He added there are no perfect kids either, but we don't expect our kids to be perfect, do we? We only expect perfection in ourselves.

Ok, you didn't do it perfectly. So what? What's to be gained by continuing to beat yourself up or to blame yourself for someone else's choices? The God whose mercies are new every morning doesn't live in the past, and neither should we (Lamentations 3:22-23).

If I waste my time replaying every past mistake I've made, I'm going to be filled with sorrow and regret and without hope because I can't change the past. Neither can you. To use our energy worrying about the future is equally as futile (Matthew 6:34). Besides being futile, it's exhausting because we can't carry tomorrow's problems with today's strength. It just doesn't work that way.

And guess what. You don't need to do either of those things. If you know for certain you did something wrong, confess it, claim God's promise of forgiveness, and let it go. Then determine in your heart, by God's grace, you will try from this day on to give God everything you have for as long as you have.

You still won't be the perfect parent, the perfect spouse or the perfect Christian, but you don't have to be. God knows what you've had to overcome just to get to where you are. He knows what life has handed you and that you are a "bruised reed." And in Isaiah 42:3, God says He will not "break a bruised reed." You can trust Him with your past, your broken heart, and your prodigal. He knows all if it already, and He knows when your heart's desire is to do what's right.

The Israelites had a saying, much like our "the apple doesn't fall very far from the tree." They would say, "the fathers have eaten sour grapes, and the children's teeth are set on edge" (Ezekiel 18:2). Through the prophet Ezekiel, God said they weren't going to be able to use that proverb any more.

Ezekiel went on to say, speaking for the Lord, "all souls are mine." But it shouldn't have been news to the Israelites. Back in Deuteronomy 24, when God was laying out a roadmap for living and for personal accountability, He covered it. He said fathers weren't to be held accountable and put to death for the sins of the sons. God held individuals responsible for their own choices then, and He still does.

Bottom line? You're not to blame. And neither are the teachers, the friends, the spouse (or even the ex-spouse), the pastor, or the youth group leader. The reason our loved ones are acting out has nothing to do with you or me or those others. It has everything to do with them, the condition of their own hearts, their relationship with God, and the decisions they have made and continue to make.

You may have said or thought or done some things you need make right. We all have. However, the choices of your prodigal are not on the list.

Something to Think About:

Is it possible your prodigal is responsible for his or her own choices?

PART TWO

A New Look at the Story of the Prodigal

"A certain man had two sons" (Luke 15:11).

At a time when I was feeling overwhelmed by what was going on in my own life and the life of my prodigal, a friend suggested I read the Luke 15 story of the prodigal son as though I had never seen it before. He added I should try to see what each person in the prodigal's family did and didn't do. I followed his suggestion and was both encouraged and challenged by what I learned. As I share those things, I hope they will encourage and challenge you as well.

The first thing I saw was they were a family. We don't know a lot about the prodigal's family except they appeared to be comfortable financially. No absent father, no food stamps, no family crisis like divorce or unemployment. None of those things society blames for the choices of our prodigals or our prodigals use as an excuse for their behavior.

Theirs was just an average family, not very different from ours, and they were in for some tough times. While our knowledge of the prodigal and his family is limited, we understand the tough times, don't we?

Since Jesus was talking to men, it makes sense the prodigal's mom wasn't included in the parable. But you and I both know her heart must have been broken as well. Our sons touch our hearts in ways no other relationships do. And she must have been devastated.

One thing of note is none of them let the choices of the prodigal destroy their family. Keeping a family together and functioning as a unit isn't easy under the best of circumstances. It becomes almost impossible when our hearts are broken. Those are the times when we tend to get trapped into blaming ourselves, other family members, and even God for the outrageous behavior of our prodigal.

How is your family handling the reality of having and loving a prodigal? Is it being torn apart from the inside because of the actions of someone you love? It doesn't have to be that way. In the midst of our suffering, which may be long, we can remember we are a family, and we can be sensitive enough to realize our whole family is hurting. The Bible prodigal's family survived, and so can ours. Having laid that foundation, let's take a look at the story and the people involved.

We will be looking at the prodigal, the father, and the older brother in this story about an average family that acted in most unusual ways. As I meditated on the behavior of each of them, I couldn't help but see the parallels between the prodigal's family and my own. I think you'll see some similarities too. The first person we will look at is the prodigal himself.

The Prodigal

He asked for what was his or someday would
become his own, and so his father gave…
although he knew the path his son might choose
could take him captive, make of him a slave.
Yet still he gave his younger son the choice.
I wonder if he let his fears give voice.

And then the wayward son went far away
from home and hearth and all things good and pure
unto a foreign land and life of sin,
and never gave his home another thought, I'm sure,
'til broken in the ashes of despair,
he stood alone and lost with none to care.

And coming to himself at last, he saw
the wisdom of the law he'd scorned and more.
With broken heart, he looked at what he'd lost,
the emptiness his future held in store.
Then his heart turned homeward, and he went
to seek his father's face and to repent.

Expecting he would earn some coins somehow
to pay his debt, he trudged along the way.
He had no cause for hope of any kind
for mercy from the Dad he left that day.
But though he went home looking just for bread,
his found forgiveness and his father's love instead.

Chapter 3
A New Look at the Prodigal

The Far Country: "the younger of them said, 'Father, give me the portion of goods that falleth to me'" (Luke 15:12).

In Bible times, the older son was entitled to a double portion of his father's inheritance, and the younger son received only one portion. However, neither of them was entitled to anything as long as their father was alive. Keep in mind, in their culture, the father ruled with absolute authority, and his word was law.

I had to smile at the nerve of the younger son, who went to his father and asked for such an outrageous thing! And he didn't even duck after he asked? A father from that time and culture was more likely to be part of the "I'll *knock* you out" group rather than the "time out" group!

The younger son was like that kid we all know. He was full of charm and wit, going from one hilarious predicament to another, making everyone laugh and shake their heads. He would be the kid we find amusing while being glad he belongs to someone else. And, of course, sometimes that rascal belongs to us.

Behavior and escapades, which made us laugh when our children were young, lose their charm when our kids get a little older and go too far. We stop seeing any humor in it when our son or daughter begins to make wrong choices and

35

walks away from us like the prodigal in our story walked away.

It was possible for the inheritance to be divided before the father's death. But the prodigal's asking was disrespectful and insulting, and I doubt his father was amused. However, the father gave his son the inheritance he asked for.

No reason is given for why the father did what the prodigal asked. Perhaps the dad was more indulgent toward his younger son. Maybe he was tired of the fight. We understand that kind of tired, don't we? Whatever the reason, he did as the prodigal asked.

Soon after he received his inheritance, the younger son turned it all into cash and headed off "to a far country." Selling his inheritance was forbidden under Jewish law, and the prodigal would have known it was. But then he took it even further.

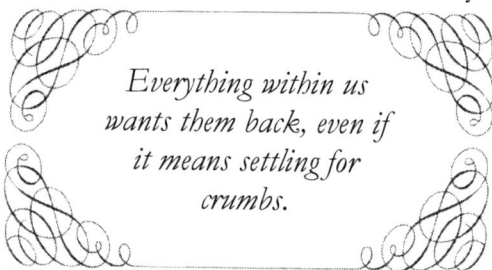

Everything within us wants them back, even if it means settling for crumbs.

Like so many young people after him, he didn't use money or freedom responsibly. However, his irresponsible behavior had started long before he headed to the far country. He began by asking his dad to do something out of the norm and alien to his culture. And in asking, he showed he already had a sense of entitlement. It also showed a lack of respect for Jewish law and customs. Oh, yes! This kid was in trouble long before the harlots, the riotous living, and the pigs.

You already know the rest of the story. He wasted the inheritance he had asked his father for and had received. We don't know how long it took him to use up his inheritance, but eventually all the money was gone. Gone too were the extravagant lifestyle and all the things his father's money had paid for. He had spent it all.

When he had "spent all," a famine came, and not just a small, every-day famine. It was a "mighty famine," and he began to "be in want" (Luke 5:14). He was destitute and alone, with no one to help him because his freeloading "friends" had disappeared when the money did.

Sadly, this story is only too familiar to those of us who love a prodigal. We've done everything we could for them, made sure they had the things they needed, and given them chance after chance after chance. Like the father in the story, we've even given in to unreasonable demands, hoping our prodigals would figure it out. Then we've watched helplessly as they threw it all away along with every opportunity to get things right.

Now a mighty famine has come into our prodigal's life, and we don't know what to do. Our hearts are broken from his choices and the consequences of them, and we are often overcome with fear about what will happen next.

The journey of the prodigal didn't end with the famine. The story wasn't finished yet. God wasn't finished in his life, and He isn't finished in the lives of our prodigals. When trouble comes, my first response is often to wonder if God has forgotten my prodigal or me. Maybe it's your response as well. However, it may be the very time God is working in our prodigal's life and in our own.

In his book, *The Problem with Pain,* C.S. Lewis wrote, "Pain insists upon being attended to. God whispers to us in our pleasures, speaks in our consciences, but shouts in our pain."[3] The Bible prodigal could not hear God's whisper in his pleasure, nor could he hear God speak in his conscience. But God was going to shout to him in his pain, and it was a shout the prodigal would hear.

Is everything falling apart in your prodigal's life? Your prodigal's disappointment and your own may be God's appointment for both of you. It could be God is using your prodigal's crisis to get his or her attention. And the story isn't finished yet.

The Famine: "And when he came to himself..." (Luke 15:17).

Our Bible prodigal was in serious trouble! He was alone and away from home in a far country and in the midst of a great famine. His money was gone, his friends were gone, and he had nothing to eat. Those were some pretty desperate circumstances. God was getting ready to get his attention, and He wasn't going to do it with enticing words or manipulation. He was going to do it by letting this young man face the consequences of his own choices.

Do you remember the three doors from "The Price is Right?" The contestant had to choose between what they already had or could see or choose an unknown behind one of the doors. It was a difficult choice to make, but choose they must.

Those of us who love a prodigal have choices too, but the choices aren't nearly as attractive as those offered by Bob Barker. The two options are usually to tolerate the unacceptable behavior of our prodigals or to step back and let happen what's going to happen. Stepping back might even mean we have no relationship with our prodigals at all, at least for right now.

The first choice comes with lies, abuse, and dysfunction and will no doubt include our being blamed for everything that's wrong in our prodigal's life. As unacceptable as this choice may be, some of us choose it because the other option—stepping back and setting limits on what we will tolerate or having no relationship at all—is even more unacceptable.

It's not easy to watch our prodigals struggling in the middle of the mess they've made of their lives. Many of us are hurting from the relationship being broken and the unkind, even cruel things our prodigals have said and done. Everything within us wants them back, even if it means settling for crumbs.

However, it isn't what's best for them, and it isn't what's best for us or for the rest of our family. There is no Door #3, no matter how much our heart cries out for a third door where our prodigals come home and want to do what's right. It just isn't an option right now—not while they're still acting out in destructive ways.

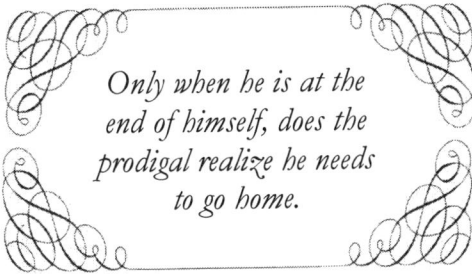

Only when he is at the end of himself, does the prodigal realize he needs to go home.

The famine was no accident. God used it to bring the prodigal to the point of despair, where "no man gave unto him" (Luke 15:16). It couldn't get much worse than feeding pigs, at least not for a Jew. What a disgraceful predicament the prodigal was in! Of all the "unclean" animals the Jews were forbidden to eat, to touch, to raise, pigs were about the worst.

Can you picture our stubborn young prodigal out in a pigsty feeding pigs? What must have been his reaction when one of them brushed against him? If you've ever seen a herd of pigs being fed, you know how they act. They climb all over each other, pushing the others out of the way, all the while grunting, squealing and making a *lot* of noise. As if that isn't enough, they smell really, really bad! And this is where the proud, selfish prodigal has found himself.

Those pigs were rubbing up against him, no doubt pushing at him with their snouts. His situation had a lot in common with clowns in a circus, both funny and tragic at the same time. And just when we think it couldn't get any worse or more humiliating, we read he would "fain have filled his belly with the husks that the swine did eat" (Luke 15:16).

Not only was he in rags and feeding pigs, but now he was hungry enough to eat their food! And when he was at the end of himself, literally starving to death, he realized his life was in shambles and he needed to go home.

I can't count the times I've "helped" my prodigals out of a crisis of their own making only to have them give away, sell, or somehow lose the things I had spent money on. I call it "buying them another relapse kit." You may have done some of the same things and, like me, done them so many times you've lost count.

We've bonded them out of jail, bought them groceries, paid their rent, paid to have their lights turned back on, or bought them another bus or plane ticket home. We've called their bosses and made excuses for them to everyone. And we've done all those things with the very best intentions.

However, doing for our prodigals what they should reasonably be doing for themselves isn't helping. Quite the opposite. And how can allowing our prodigals to verbally abuse us really be in their best interest or in our own? I'm afraid we sometimes harm rather than help our prodigals with our interference and our willingness to tolerate unacceptable behavior.

What might happen if you and I set limits on how we will allow our prodigals to treat us? What might happen if we stepped back and let happen what's going to happen instead of shielding them from the natural consequences of their choices?

A mother recently told me she disagreed with me and said, "as long as [she] had breath in her body, [she] would help her prodigal out of whatever mess he was in." It's her choice, of course. However, I have to wonder if she's getting in the way of what God is trying to do in her prodigal's life.

The Journey Back: "I will arise and go to my father" (Luke 15:18).

We won't ever see the significance of the story of the prodigal unless we see some basic truths about the prodigal and his family. For example, it's important to remember the prodigal didn't head for home because he was sorry he had hurt his family. In the beginning, the only reason he decided to go home was because he needed help.

According to Dr. Kenneth Bailey, an expert in Middle Eastern culture, the prodigal son was not repentant in the sense of being sorry for what he had done. Dr. Bailey further says the word Jesus used in the parable was "nepash," meaning he was going to depend on himself.[4]

Dr. Bailey said if the prodigal had really seen his need for repentance, Jesus would have used the word "shub," which means, "return to God."[5] Our prodigal wasn't planning to seek his father's forgiveness. He didn't yet see the awfulness of what he had done. He wanted to go back to his father's house because he was starving and eating with pigs. Being hungry got his attention. Feeding the pigs got his attention.

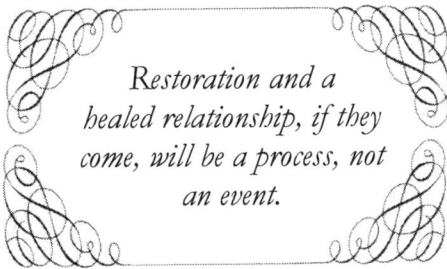

Restoration and a healed relationship, if they come, will be a process, not an event.

Those things even showed him he was in serious trouble. However, he still had a plan he thought would get him out of the predicament he was in and allow him to "save face."

From the beginning, the prodigal had thought only of himself, not caring about the pain and suffering he was causing the people who loved him. It's difficult for people from our culture to see how outrageous it was for him to ask for the inheritance while his father was alive. It was the equivalent of wishing his father dead so he could have what he wanted. Anyone who loves a prodigal will understand his callous and brutal selfishness. We've lived it. Some of us are still living it.

Can you sense the arrogance of this young man? He was hungry, but not broken, and I can almost hear him practicing the speech he's going to make to his father. With every step away from the pigpen, he became more convinced all he needed was a decent job so he could buy back the inheritance he had sold. He didn't want to return as a slave, without rights, but as a servant. A servant earned wages, so he had no intention of seeking the father's forgiveness. Repentance wasn't part of the prodigal son's plan...not at first.

He would have known Jewish culture required the community to shun him because he had wasted his inheritance in a foreign land. He had no reason to expect acceptance or forgiveness—not from his family, not from his friends, and not from his community. It was going to be a long walk home for the prodigal. I believe it was this long walk and the time he had to think that began to work in his heart.

The path back for our prodigals may be a long one as well, and we can't assume their wanting to come home implies repentance. If we have expectations about what they should think or say or do, we're setting ourselves up for disappointment. It's a journey and not theirs alone, but ours as well. It involves not only letting our prodigals hit bottom, but also remembering the homecoming may be a journey as well.

Restoration and a healed relationship, if they come, will be a process, not an event. The prodigal in our story either couldn't or wouldn't see how he had hurt his family, at least not in the beginning. And it may be our prodigals can't or won't see how they have hurt us. Until they do, we can remind ourselves not to take it personally. Our prodigals will see it someday, but it won't be until God has done the work in their lives that God alone can do.

Yes, it's going to be a long walk back for our Bible prodigal, and he has some heavy duty thinking to do on the way. Let's leave him for a while and take a look at what his father is doing back home.

Something to Think About:

Has your prodigal started to experience some natural consequences for his or her behavior? What are they?

Chapter 4
A New Look at the Father

"A certain man had two sons…" (Luke 15:11).

Any discussion of the story of the prodigal's father must take into account that father represents God. Because of that fact alone, none of us will be able to measure up to the level of love and grace he shows to his prodigal son. However, we can profit by taking a look at not only the father's broken heart, but also what he did and did not do about his prodigal son. Let's look first as some things he didn't do.

The father didn't refuse his son. In the culture of the Middle East, the father's younger son had humiliated and brought shame to his entire family before he ever left home. To ask his father for the inheritance was the same as saying, "I wish you were dead!" The reaction of a father from his culture would have been immediate, violent and final, and it would have included disowning the son. But it wasn't this father's reaction.

Then the prodigal sold his part of the property, which was also unheard of. Imagine the pain and embarrassment of his family, especially the father! He must have cringed as he watched his son do disgraceful and shameful things. And the prodigal did them in full view of his father, his family, his friends and everyone who knew them.

When you and I give into our prodigals' unreasonable requests, it's because of our human weakness. However, the father in our parable represents God, and He is anything but weak. Why would the father in the parable give his son something that would harm him?

Why would an all-knowing God give our prodigal sons and daughters something that isn't in their best interest? Why would God do that to them? To us? Why would He let us suffer like this when we as parents tried to do what was right? Why didn't He stop our prodigals from going down a wrong path? Those bitter questions are so profound—and so human.

The answer is one I already know, and so do you. God gives each of us a free will and allows us to make our own choices. Our prodigals are exercising their free will just as we do. God will not stop them or us from exercising our free will and making our own choices, even if those choices are going to hurt us and hurt the ones we love.

When any of us makes up our mind to do something, whether right or wrong, God will let us do as we choose. However, our prodigals and we ourselves will pay a price for the choices we make. Psalm 106:15 tells us about a time when Israel insisted on having their way, "And [God] gave them their request; but sent leanness into their soul."

The father didn't make his son stay home: The father in our parable didn't try to micro-manage or control his son's choices. The prodigal son must have been old enough to leave home and make his own decisions, whether right or wrong. Had he been younger, the story would have been much different.

When our kids are young and still in our home, God expects us to "chasten thy son while there is hope" (Proverbs 19:18). We can't let our children run wild, make excuses for them, or refuse to hold them accountable and then ask God what went wrong.

We also can't expect our sons and daughters to remain children forever—however much we wish they would. And when they become adults, they have the right to make their own choices…no matter how much those choices grieve our hearts. And they sometimes do.

Trying to stop this Bible prodigal would have been about as easy as trying to stop a train. But it appears the father didn't try. Maybe he realized what we struggle with every day to remember—that we can't control another human being or force a desired change. No matter how clearly we see the destruction coming, we have to let our prodigals find out for themselves whether their choices are the wrong ones.

The father didn't make excuses for his son: The father went against the customs of the time by dividing his inheritance while he was living. He would have known his doing that would bring upon him the scorn and mocking ridicule or at least the pity of the village. Later on, when his prodigal son came home, the father again broke with tradition. He wasn't controlled by what other people thought about him, his family, or his prodigal.

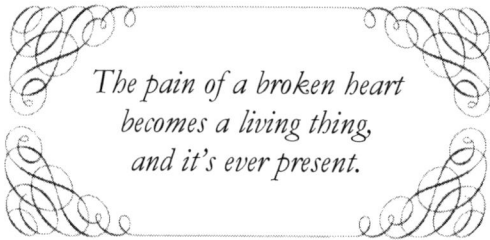

> *The pain of a broken heart becomes a living thing, and it's ever present.*

Without a doubt, the father's heart was broken as never before by the actions of his son. And when our hearts are broken over our children, it stops being about what people think or say. It stops being about "people knowing." It stops being about embarrassment or reputation or the opinion of anyone else. It's so much more than that. The pain of a broken heart becomes a living thing, and it's ever present. With a grief no one but God understands, our deepest longing becomes just to see our prodigal decide to do the right thing.

The things the father did and didn't do about his prodigal son are a reminder that we can't control anyone's behavior but our own. His part of the story also reminds us it's not our responsibility or our place to explain, make excuses for or apologize for someone else's behavior, no matter how much we love them. We are accountable only for our own choices.

One of the most heart-breaking things about loving a prodigal is the entire family is often judged by the behavior of the prodigal. While I can't make anyone think differently, I can refuse to own someone else's outrageous behavior. And I can refuse to accept as valid someone else's opinion of my prodigal, my family, my situation or myself.

I can refuse to be battered or bullied by the opinions or the criticism of people who have never walked my path. And I can be gracious and kind both to myself and to them, knowing they really don't understand.

The father didn't interfere: The prodigal's father didn't drop everything and follow his son to the far country. He took his hands off the situation and let happen whatever was going to happen.

Just letting things happen however they are going to happen may be the hardest part of loving a prodigal. Desperate, we've told ourselves our prodigals would get things right if only something would happen to get their attention. In trying to "get their attention," we've done some incredible things.

We've called the parents of their friends or gone to their homes. We've called their probation officers, their Court Referral Officers, or even the police. We've hacked their email accounts, logged in as them on Facebook, Instagram, or MySpace and followed them, sometimes borrowing a friend's car so they wouldn't recognize us. We've reported a party they were attending to the police or the Drug Task Force, or we've shown up where they were and insisted they come home. If our prodigal is in a 12-step program, we've even called his sponsor.

What's wrong with trying to "help" our prodigals see what could happen? Many things are wrong with that kind of "helping," not the least of which is it will steal our serenity. We won't have any kind of peace as long as we're trying to manipulate the situation or the outcome. And it's not our fight. According to 1 Samuel 17:47, "the battle is the Lord's." It's not my battle, and it's not yours. It's a spiritual battle, and we don't determine the outcome. God does.

The root cause of those ways of "helping" is fear, an emotion with which we are all too familiar. Oh, yes. We know about fear, don't we? However, giving in to fear by doing the kinds of things listed here doesn't ease our fear. It feeds and intensifies it. We can't fix anyone and, despite our best intentions, it's futile to try. Think about the times you've struggled to fix yourself. If you and I can't do that, why would we think we can fix anyone else?

The father didn't bail his son out: We've bailed our kids out a time or two, haven't we? It isn't easy to watch the people we love suffer as their lives are falling apart, and I'm sure it was just as true of the father in our parable.

No level of degradation is lower for a Jew than to be feeding pigs, and it's where the prodigal was. We see no indication he let his father know where he was or how low he had fallen, but I don't believe he ended up in the pigsty the day after he spent everything. It took some time, and the journey couldn't have been an easy one as his life fell apart bit by bit. Yet at no time did the father shield his prodigal from the natural consequences he was facing. Neither should we.

"But I love him!" Of course you do, and I love my prodigal too. However, sometimes our "helping" isn't helping at all, and our interference is hurting rather than helping our prodigal. Those of us who have been doing this for a while have found an easy tool for evaluating whether or not it's a good idea for us to "help." All we have to do is ask ourselves one simple

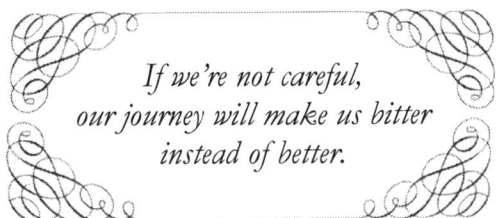

> *If we're not careful, our journey will make us bitter instead of better.*

question, "Am I doing for my prodigal what he or she should reasonably be doing for themselves?"

I don't mean what our prodigals could do if they weren't drinking, on drugs, or just fired from yet another job. I'm talking about whether it's reasonable for us to pay the electric bill for a 35-year-old man, who is healthy and strong and who should be able to pay it himself.

Healthy love helps rather than hurts an individual. I've known many young people in half-way houses, who said they knew their parents loved them. I've lost count of the number of those kids who added, "They almost loved me to death."

Most of us who love a prodigal spend a great deal of time worrying about things we can't change or control. We spend days and weeks and months fighting battles, which are not ours, and then wonder why we're exhausted. What would it feel like to take our hands off and let God do things in His way and in His time? We can't do that if we're being controlled by fear. Maybe it's time to ask God to soothe those fears and to remind us the battle is His.

The father didn't give up: "Weeping may endure for a night, but joy cometh in the morning" (Psalm 30:5).

Can you picture the pain in the father's face as he watched his son start down a road he knew couldn't possibly end well? Forget his son had a sense of entitlement to things for which he had never worked. Forget this selfish boy had no intention of being available to help his parents as they aged. Forget the prodigal had left every responsibility for his older brother to handle alone.

Forget those things and just think for a moment of the father's broken heart and your own. If you're walking this path, you know what I'm talking about. We've watched our prodigals ignore our pleas and our tears. We've watched them walk away, not seeming to care if our hearts were in shreds and tears were streaming down our face.

The life verse of a pastor friend is 3 John 1:4, which says, "I have no greater joy than to hear that my children walk in truth." I'm sure it's true for my friend. But it's also true there is perhaps no greater despair than that of a parent whose son or daughter has rejected them and everything they stand for and has chosen a life of sin and rebellion against God. It hurts. And it doesn't just hurt a little. It hurts a lot.

It isn't easy to hold on to hope when your heart has been broken and every plan and dream you had for your prodigal is in ashes. I've felt hopeless, and you have too—so overcome with loss and fear and disappointment, it was like being in a wilderness and seeing no way out. Nothing can compare with the desperate and lonely grief of our midnight hour in the wilderness.

It's ok and even necessary to grieve in our midnight hour. But we can cling to this assurance: morning is coming in our lives and in the lives of our prodigals. And when morning comes, it will bring joy of a kind you and I can't even imagine today.

While we're in the wilderness, we can remember we're not alone. In spite of what it looks like to us and in spite of what we're feeling, we can choose to believe our God is faithful. And we can refuse to give up hope. Is the wilderness overwhelming? Oh, yes. But it's temporary. You and I aren't going to be in the wilderness forever.

I know you're weary. I'm sometimes weary too. But we can rest and lean on the arm of a God who loves us and who will support us on our journey in the wilderness. God is faithful, and He won't leave you or me alone in the wilderness we're facing. The day will come, I promise it will, when people will say, "Who is this that cometh up from the wilderness, leaning on her beloved?" (Song of Solomon 8:5).

While there were several things the father in our parable did not do, there were also some things he did. Let's look at a few of them.

The father took care of himself: "But when he was yet a great way off, his father saw him, and had compassion, and ran…" (Luke 15:20).

Now how can we know the father took care of himself from such a small portion of Scripture? We can know this for the same reason we know he was not in poor health or near death when the prodigal asked for his inheritance. When the prodigal returned home, the father didn't hobble out to meet him leaning on his walker…he RAN! And he didn't run five feet or one block. Scripture tells us he saw his son coming while he was "a great way off."

I have some friends who have done and are doing the "Couch to 5K" challenge, and they would tell you running isn't for sissies! No matter how much joy and relief flooded the father's heart when he saw his son, he couldn't have run a "great way" if he had been a physical wreck. He couldn't have done it if he had spent the months or maybe even years his prodigal had been in the far country neglecting his health.

It can be a challenge to take care of ourselves when someone we love is acting out. It isn't easy to eat when we

51

have no appetite or to sleep when our minds are consumed with worry or grief. And I'm not going to say you will need your strength to run and embrace your prodigal when he comes home. I can't promise when he or she will come home because I don't know God's plan for your prodigal or even for my own.

The father in the parable didn't know the end of the story, so his taking care of himself had nothing to do with the prodigal. It had everything to do with the father recognizing his own value and knowing he had the right and the responsibility to take care of himself.

Just because our prodigal is acting out, making the wrong choices, doing the wrong thing doesn't mean we have to turn into a martyr. If we're not careful, those of us who love a prodigal will find ourselves riding our pity pony all the way to Alaska and back and neglecting the basic things we need to do to take care of ourselves. If we choose not to take care of ourselves, it isn't our prodigal who is hurting us. We're doing it to ourselves.

What can we do instead? We can focus on taking care of ourselves. We can eat when it's time to eat, we can sleep when it's time to sleep, and we can go to the doctor like we should. The wilderness path we walk when we love a prodigal isn't an easy one, and we will need every bit of strength we can muster. We won't have those reserves if we are neglecting the basic things we need to do to take care of ourselves.

Taking care of ourselves physically can be the first step toward taking care of ourselves in other important ways. Have you been doing the routine things like going to the doctor, the dentist or the gym? Can you take a hard look at areas you are neglecting and then determine to take care of one of them today?

The father did what he would usually do: "Live joyfully...for that is thy portion in this life, and in thy labour which thou takest under the sun" (Ecclesiastes 9:9).

For as long as I've known the story of the prodigal, I've pictured the father with one hand shielding his eyes as he watched the road and waited for the return of his son. I was certain his life stopped the minute his son broke his heart and left home. I assumed the father spent his days brooding and watching for his son, finding no joy or purpose in his life unless and until his son came home.

Careful reading of the parable, however, in the context of the culture doesn't support that. Those people were farmers. They had crops and animals and land, and all those things require work—outside work. I believe it's what he was doing when he looked up and saw his son a "great way off."

The prodigal would have been reluctant to enter the village where he was an outcast, so it's even possible the father may have seen his son standing on the outskirts of the village. The father could have been going about his business in the village or sitting at the gate with the elders. Whether he was tending crops and animals, attending to business in the village, or sitting with the elders, he was doing something more than just waiting for his prodigal's return. Regardless of his broken heart and the broken relationship, he busied himself about the business of living his life.

So should we. Trying to focus on living our lives and finding joy aren't easy things to do. The difficulty is multiplied when our relationship is broken with the people we love most in the world—our children, our spouses or any of the rest of our family. However, Ecclesiastes 9:9 admonishes us to live joyfully, and it goes on to say this is our "portion under the sun." It's a gift from God. We don't need to sacrifice our entire lives and all the other people we love on the altar of our prodigals or even on the altar of our own broken hearts. Our sorrow is a part of our lives, and no one would suggest otherwise. But it doesn't have to be the whole.

Will your heart and mine be heavy sometimes because of our prodigals? Of course, they will. We're just human, and grief or sadness and even a broken heart are all valid feelings when you love a prodigal. But they are just feelings—nothing more—and they don't have to dictate what we think, what we say, or what we do. Regardless of our circumstances or the broken relationships, our prodigals can steal our joy only if we let them.

I have found by bitter experience that when I use up all my emotional reserves grieving my broken relationships, I have no energy left to find joy in the ones that are whole. Those relationships with people I love and who love me are one of God's gifts—my "portion under the sun." And those sweet relationships are your "portion under the sun" as well.

It can be empowering when we begin to take back bits and pieces of our lives—those things of joy, which we've given up because of our prodigal's behavior and the problems associated with or caused by that behavior. When we're back in church, back in the choir, doing volunteer work at the animal shelter, reading a good book, working in our garden or taking a long walk, we'll find joy again. Joy is everywhere around us, and it's available to us if we're willing to open our eyes. When we look for it, we'll find the wonder in every day even if every day isn't wonderful.

What have you stopped doing because of your prodigal? What are the blessings you're missing and the joy you're giving up? Whether it's working in your garden, playing with your grandchildren, taking a class or just going out to lunch with a friend, taking action to reclaim a small part of your life will go a long way toward giving you back your joy.

The father really saw his prodigal: "his father saw him" (Luke 15:20).

I recognize the father of the prodigal represents God, and we can't begin to show the same depth of compassion and forgiveness. However, we can still learn some things from what he did. The first thing we can learn is the father really "saw" him.

A pastor friend once told me the reason parents have a hard time setting limits and continue to shield their kids from consequences is they don't see their kids clearly. Looking through a parent's eyes, they see their baby taking his first steps and reaching out to his mom or dad. If it's a prodigal husband, the wife remembers the love they used to share. And all of us remember better times.

My friend was right; our prodigal isn't the same as he was. In fact, some of us who love a prodigal may wonder if the person we loved even exists anymore. It's hard to reconcile the person they were with the person they seem to be now.

But I would suggest that after our prodigals have been acting out for a while, we also don't see them clearly. It isn't easy to look beyond our hurt, our tears, and our anger to see the person we love trapped in a cage and to feel compassion, especially since he has fashioned the cage himself. However, it's what the father saw. If we are going to make a difference in anyone's life—our prodigal's life, the lives of others, or our own, we will need to see our prodigal differently too.

For the father to have held his robe up in his hand and run was unheard of in his culture, and the father brought more ridicule and shame on his family and himself by doing it. What his community expected and would have respected is for him to turn his back on his prodigal son and declare him dead. Since the father later said his son "had been dead," he no doubt felt some anger and resentment himself at one point. But when he saw his son, his anger was changed to compassion.

The younger son had changed. We talk about letting our prodigals "hit bottom," and as far as bottoms go, this was about as far down as it could get. When the father saw—I mean really saw—his lost and broken son, he was moved with compassion and remembered the love he felt for his lost son. And it didn't matter to him what the community thought or what his friends thought. His son was coming home.

No doubt you're hoping I will say your showing the same kind of love will make your prodigal come home or at least want to come home. But I can't say it will. Our prodigal's homecoming and the change of heart needed to bring it about aren't up to us. It's a work God needs to do. But we make a grave mistake when we assume our prodigal is the only one who needs the touch of God. They need to change and grow, but so do we.

When one person in the family begins to act out, the whole family gets sick. So our prodigals aren't the only ones who need a touch from God. Any serenity and peace of mind we once had are usually a thing of the past. If you and I want to regain our peace and have the serenity we say we want, God will have to take our anger, our resentments, and our offended pride and teach us to be "kind, tender-hearted, and forgiving" (Ephesians 4:32).

Are you holding on to anger and resentment? I know I was. And the answer for this heartbroken parent was to forget about "fixing" my prodigal and to focus instead on what God wanted me to learn from the entire terrible situation. I didn't begin to find peace until I stopped asking God *how* I could get out of my circumstances and started instead asking *what* I could get out of them.

The father had compassion: "his father...had compassion" (Luke 15:20).

We fostered a rescue dog, a Papillon named Mike. When Mike first came to live with us, we were appalled to hear what his living conditions had been in a "puppy mill" kennel the state closed down. He may have been the filthiest animal I have ever seen before or since. And it was no wonder. He had lived his life in a cage with a wire mesh bottom, and it was where he ate and slept and relieved himself. The closest thing to a bath he had ever had was when the cages were sprayed with a high-pressure hose.

He had never walked on grass, chased a squirrel, been given a treat, or seen a butterfly for which his breed is named. It wasn't the way Mike's life stared out. He had a loving mother, who I'm sure nursed him and cleaned him and protested vigorously when he was snatched away from her and put in a cage by cruel hands.

Mike isn't like other dogs. Our vet said he suffers from a severe case of "kennel-itis," which is easy to understand, given what he's experienced. We've had to set limits on his behavior, but it had to be done gently and repeatedly, with the kind of patience and compassion he needed and deserved.

He has never been mean or vicious and has made progress, but it has been a slow process. When he first came to live with us, we had to coax him out of his kennel. He was so far from his mother's love it wasn't even a distant memory anymore. Captivity was the only thing he knew, and the world outside his cage was a huge and very scary place. He couldn't even imagine himself walking through the door of that kennel and being free.

If we could really see our prodigal and the hopelessness he feels or the loneliness of the cage he has put himself in, I don't think the compassion would be long in coming. The prodigal's father not only saw his son, but he also saw his son's lost, hopeless state. And seeing his son this way is where the compassion came from.

As tough as it is to love a prodigal, I'm convinced it's even harder to be a prodigal. For all their bluff and bravado, I know a part of them mourns the loss of the relationships they had with those of us who love and grieve them most. Their losses are as great as ours, and I sometimes think their losses are even greater.

I'm not saying we should continue to enable our prodigals by shielding them from the natural consequences of their choices. Nor am I suggesting we tolerate abuse or outrageous behavior. I've known parents who refused to press charges when their prodigals stole their cars or even physically abused them. If we choose to allow those things, it's not helping us or our prodigal. But reacting from a mind-set of anger or retaliation isn't going to help them or us either.

Loving a prodigal means we have a tough journey ahead of us, and we're going to be hurt along the way. If we're not careful, our journey will make us bitter instead of better. Or we can ask God to give us the compassion we need to have for our prodigals and their helpless state.

If you and I are without compassion, it isn't the prodigal who's responsible. What is your heart like today? Is it filled with compassion or with anger, resentment and bitterness? Can you try to see your prodigal the way God sees him...locked in a cage and unable to see the open door?

You might be thinking, "But I'm so angry!" Anger is a natural emotion and one with which you're no doubt familiar if you have a prodigal. I still have days when I'm angry. When the bills aren't being paid, when the curfews aren't being respected, when we've just found out the latest outrageous thing our prodigals have done, anger is both natural and appropriate. And when we're frightened, hurt and angry, it's hard to remember compassion and mercy.

As I've read and reread the story of the prodigal son in order to write about it, I've seen my prodigal over and over. You've probably seen your prodigal too. How could we not? But I've also seen myself in the pain of the father.

We've been where the father is in the story as we've watched our prodigals defiantly rebel against everything we stand for and against the God we love. We've watched them selfishly demand all we can give them and more and then walk away from us. We've even watched them go off to a "far country," so far removed from what's good and clean and right, they might as well have been thousands of miles away. How can we get past the anger and into a frame of mind where we can feel compassion?

Luke 15 doesn't tell us the father was patient, longsuffering, or indifferent to the outrageous things his son had done. It was not trivial in his Jewish culture for the father to say his son had been "dead." Everything the son had done justified his father disowning him and declaring him dead. It may sound like a very hard stand, but I've been hurt and angry enough to at least think that. Haven't you? However, when the prodigal's father saw him—I mean really saw him—he was moved with compassion.

Our prodigal's path isn't about us. It never was.

Compassion is a sympathetic concern, seeing the suffering or pain of another person and feeling pity for them. It's realizing that even if our prodigal deserved to lose his wife, his family and everything he loved, it's heartbreaking to see it happen. Compassion is realizing consequences hurt, even if our prodigals brought them on themselves, and knowing they did this to themselves makes them hurt more, not less. Compassion will enable us to forgive our prodigals when it is in our power to hurt or punish or strike back at them.

Compassion doesn't mean we can't or shouldn't hold our prodigals accountable because we can, and we should. In fact, the father of the prodigal didn't give his younger son another portion of his property. He had been given his share, and losing it was his problem. We can learn from his example. If our prodigals are in debt, they need to be the ones to pay it back. If they wrecked their car, it's not our job to replace it. However, if we find joy or satisfaction in seeing their house of cards fall down, it isn't our prodigals who have the problem.

If we could really see how lost and alone our prodigals are, how frightened, how desperate, compassion wouldn't be a stretch for us. If drugs or alcohol are involved, those prodigals are in captivity to something much bigger than they. And if they could stop for the parents, the wife, the kids, or anyone at all, they would.

Our prodigal's path isn't about us. It never was. It's about them and their relationship with God, and their journey is a painful one. It isn't easy to look beyond our own pain and see the pain of our prodigals, is it? However, if we could imagine, if only for a moment, how it must hurt to be estranged from everyone they love, our hearts would be broken for our prodigals. If we could really see their pain, we would have no problem feeling compassion.

A friend shared with me a story about her prodigal, which illustrates what I'm saying. This prodigal is still living with her parents, and her mom was giving her a ride home from work. She knew her daughter had been drinking again, and the mother's hurt and disappointment were so great, they stole her voice and caused her to be silent. That mother wasn't angry; she was devastated and trying to hold back her tears. But hurt sometimes steals our voices too, doesn't it?

The daughter went immediately to her room when they arrived home. Then she came out and, with tears streaming down her face, entreated her mother, "Mom, please don't get so angry you won't talk to me! You don't know how much I'm suffering or how hard I'm trying!"

I believe that young woman was sincere both in the pain she felt from thinking her mom was angry at her and also in her shame and sorrow at the entire situation. Most prodigals aren't as self-aware or honest as my friend's daughter. However, even when they cover their sorrow and shame with anger or indifference, you can believe it's right under the surface. And if you can see that much pain in someone you love, how can you not feel compassion?

Something to Think About:

Do you spend a lot of time feeling angry and resentful at your prodigal? Is it helpful in any way?

Chapter 5
A New Look at the Homecoming

The prodigal: "And the son said unto him, Father, I have sinned against heaven, and in thy sight, and am no more worthy to be called thy son" (Luke 15:21).

When we left the prodigal a few pages ago to talk about the father, the prodigal was headed home. He had practiced the manipulative speech he was going to make to his dad, one that would let him "save face" and get him a job. "Make me as one of your servants" could be summarized by saying, "Look—I'm in a bit of a financial bind, but it's nothing I can't handle. I just need a job so I can fix this mess." At least that's how the trip started.

The journey back from the far country was at least as long as the journey there had been. He didn't get to the far country in one day, and it's certain he didn't get back home in one day either. And along the way, he had time to think. It was just the prodigal and the Holy Spirit of God.

Dad wasn't preaching or yelling at him, his older brother wasn't telling him what a loser he was, and his mom wasn't trying to help him or nag or make the trip back home easier. Each of them was busy doing what they needed to be doing and leaving the process and the journey of the prodigal to him and to God alone.

Taking our hands off isn't easy to do, is it? We find ourselves thinking, "if only the right person would talk to him or if the police knew what he was doing and arrested him, he'd get the picture." When we think about how terrible the end of our prodigal's path could be, we're filled with fear and desperation. And when we know how low the bottom can be for our prodigals, who could blame us for wanting to intervene if we can?

But the simplest and wisest advice I've ever received is the combined advice of two friends. It was also the most difficult to practice. One told me, "You are not the one who can help your prodigal, so take off the God cloak. Your prodigal has a God, and it's not you." The other friend said, "Why don't you let the legal system do what it does, let God do what God does, and you just take your hands off and start taking care of yourself?"

Being told I was not the one who could influence or help my prodigal first angered me and then it broke my heart. I spent weeks feeling hurt by my friends' straightforward counsel, even though I knew they both loved me. But I eventually saw the wisdom of what they said.

Our prodigals are not going to experience a life change from a changed heart because we have bullied, pleaded or manipulated them into it. The kind of change they need is going to come only from the work of God's Holy Spirit in their lives. It might happen at a church or a treatment center or a meeting of Alcoholics Anonymous. It might even be in a jail cell or in a wilderness experience that breaks our hearts as much as it breaks theirs. The point is this is God's work, not ours.

Are you desperately trying to control the outcome for your prodigal? Aren't you exhausted from trying to "fix" him? Have you pleaded and prayed and tried to influence him or her to no avail? I know I did. And the main reason we're exhausted is because we're trying to do what we were never intended to do. Our prodigals have a Holy Spirit, and it's not me, and it's not you.

If we can't "fix" the situation (and we can't), what can we do? We can give our prodigals to a faithful God, who loves them more than we do and who does not fail. Then we can let the situation go, trusting God to work it out in His way and in His time.

On the surface, it seems like what the prodigal said to his father was the same manipulative speech he had practiced. But if we look closely, part of it is missing. The missing part was asking for a job. He didn't ask his father to "Make me as one of your servants."

Somehow, somewhere on his journey home, the prodigal son came to terms with what he had done, how terrible it was. With new insight, all he wanted was to repent and be in a restored relationship with his dad. What a heartbreaking picture to see him standing alone, filthy from feeding swine and from his journey, dressed in rags, hungry and broken, and only wanting to come home. And he asked for nothing.

What finally broke the prodigal's will and caused him to repent? In order to understand the answer, we need to take a look at what the father did when his prodigal returned.

The father: "But when he was yet a great way off, his father saw him, and had compassion, and ran, and fell on his neck, and kissed him...the father said to his servants, Bring forth the best robe, and put it on him; and put a ring on his hand, and shoes on his feet" (Luke 15:20, 22).

The prodigal's stubborn will was not broken in the far country. Even though he was dressed in rags and feeding pigs, he was telling himself his problems were just financial. He was going to ask his dad for a job so he could get himself out of the mess he was in. He had a plan, and it didn't include humbling himself or admitting he had done anything wrong.

Our prodigals usually have a plan too. With their magical thinking, they talk about how they are going to "fix" their lives. They're going to buy and sell houses to make a lot of money, they're going to get a manager's position, or they're going to find the "right" person, and everything will be ok.

Of course, those things don't fix the problem because our prodigal's problem isn't the money or the job or being with the wrong person. Nor were these the problems with the prodigal in our parable. Just as with our prodigals, his was a spiritual problem, and his solution couldn't be found in the "Help Wanted" section of the newspaper or on Craig's List or on match.com.

I wonder when he began to see the holes in his plan. Was it on the long journey home, or did he come face to face with his dilemma on the outskirts of his village? He couldn't have expected to be welcomed by his village, by his family, and especially not by his father.

He may have deceived himself for a while about how he was going to walk through the village with his head held high. But at some point, he began to see things from a different perspective. Would he be shunned or ridiculed or worse? He had disgraced his entire family and brought shame to his village. He could have and should have been permanently banished when he returned.

But that isn't what happened. When the father saw his prodigal son a long way off, he threw off all dignity and forgot about appearances. He grabbed up his robes, held them with his hand or with his teeth and ran to embrace the son who had come home. The father "fell on his neck, and kissed him." And he didn't just kiss him once. The Greek word here is "katephilesen." It means he kissed him over and over again.

We have a new grandbaby named Hanna. When I first saw her at the hospital, she was sleeping, and I told my son, "I can't wait for her to wake up so I can kiss her all over her little face!" That's what happened when the father embraced the prodigal. He kissed him "all over his face."

And his son wasn't a cute little baby smelling like powder and all the sweet little baby smells. This was his prodigal son, the one who had broken his heart and humiliated him, who smelled like pigs, filthy clothes, sweat, and travel.

The prodigal's stubborn will may or may not have been close to broken before his father took the first step to run and "fall on his neck." But I believe the final eye opener for our

Bible prodigal was seeing the unconditional love of his father, who embraced him, filthy rags and all. What finally broke him? I believe it was his father's unwavering, broken-hearted and sacrificial love.

When the prodigal was broken, and I mean *really* broken, his father fully restored him to the family. By putting on his son the "finest robe," which would have been the father's own, he made a stand the community would have to accept. Wearing the father's ring gave his son the authority to do business on behalf of his father. The shoes meant he was not a slave, but a son. His son, who had been lost, was now found and restored. The prodigal had come home.

Something to Think About:

Are you harboring anger and resentment in your heart? What can you do about it?

Chapter 6
A New Look at the Older Brother

"And he was angry, and would not go in: therefore came his father out, and intreated him. And he answering said to his father, Lo, these many years do I serve thee, neither transgressed I at any time thy commandment" (Luke 15:28-29).

Our study of the prodigal and his family would not be complete without taking a look at the older brother and his relationship with his father. The Scripture tells us this older brother came back from working in the field and heard the sounds of a party going on. I have to wonder why he asked a servant what was happening instead of going inside to see for himself.

We can't know for sure, but we can conclude from our own experiences that the family hadn't done much celebrating since the younger brother had left. So the older brother could make an educated guess of his own about why they were suddenly having a party.

This poor father didn't win the lottery when it came to sons, did he? The younger one had wished him dead, demanded his inheritance, and broken his heart. Now when their culture required the older son be a part of the celebration and serve his father's guests, his son is having a temper tantrum in the courtyard and refusing to come inside.

By his behavior, he had insulted the guests and humiliated his father. One might say, "rebellious sons: the gift that keeps on giving." Two perspectives can be found here, the father's and the older son's. And we can learn some things from both.

The father: The father's response to his older son was not the expected one. Instead of rebuking his defiant son, the father went outside and "intreated him." He didn't make excuses for the prodigal, and he didn't apologize for restoring his prodigal son to the family. He didn't owe his older son an apology, and he didn't give one. He simply told him it was "meet" or fitting for them to be celebrating. And he was right.

We have reason to celebrate when our prodigals come home, and we don't need to be on the defensive about it with our family or friends. The prodigal's father didn't deny the accusations, defend the prodigal or make excuses for him. Nor should he have. Neither did the father lie for his prodigal or cover up what he had done.

It's not easy to find the balance with other members of the family when you love a prodigal. If you're like me, you sometimes find yourself explaining your prodigal to the rest of your family and the rest of your family to your prodigal. I know the only person I can control is myself. Yet knowing it doesn't stop me from trying, like some master puppeteer, to work both parts of a relationship when it doesn't even include me. It would be amusing if it weren't so sad.

But the father in our parable seemed to find a balance. He didn't reject his older son because that son wasn't willing to forgive and accept his younger brother. The father met his older son where he was and loved and embraced him whether he was willing to forgive his brother or not.

Neither did he bring the prodigal to the brother to "fix" the relationship. He left it up to them to figure it out between themselves and without his interference. What a novel idea! Instead of exhausting ourselves trying to "fix" the relationships of others in our family, we could try to love all of them where they are. What a relief it would be if we could just take a step back and let them figure out their relationship or lack of one for themselves.

The brother: I can understand the older brother's jealousy, anger, and resentment and even his refusing to come in and be part of the celebration. I can agree he seems to have "served" his father for "these many years."

Compared to his prodigal brother, he looks pretty good, doesn't he? But to say, "neither transgressed I at any time thy commandment..." (Luke 15:29)? Never? Not even once? What he said implies perfection. Do you know anyone who is always right and always chooses to do the right thing? Neither do I. That kind of perfection isn't just unlikely, it's impossible. A super spiritual phrase comes to mind here: Hogwash!

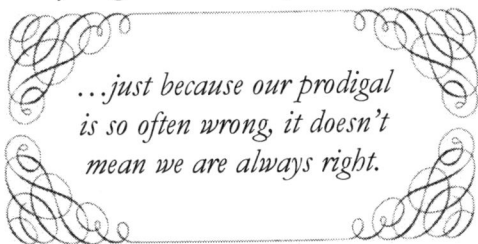

...just because our prodigal is so often wrong, it doesn't mean we are always right.

During one of the class sessions I teach in the Court Referral Program, we discuss how substance abuse affects not only the person who is abusing drugs or alcohol, but also the entire family. When one person in the family is acting out, the entire family stops functioning effectively. And the prodigal isn't the only one who is in denial when it happens. If we're not careful, those of us who live with the insanity of loving a prodigal will stop seeing our situations and ourselves the way they or we really are.

When a prodigal is acting out, it creates chaos in a family because destructive behavior doesn't happen in a vacuum. People are hurt, hearts are broken, and relationships are damaged. All of us who have been through this or are going through it now have no problem seeing the prodigal has a problem.

However, it's more difficult to see we might also have a problem. After all, we're the responsible ones. We're the ones who are trying to do the right thing. We're the ones going to church, taking a job to help pay the bills, and raising our children without any help.

If we are harsh or unreasonable, even cruel in the things we say or do to or about our prodigal, we might say it isn't without provocation. However, while we may be right about being provoked, we would be dead wrong if we think our prodigal's behavior justifies our actions or reactions. This is where I remind you and myself that just because our prodigal is often wrong, it doesn't mean we are always right.

Continue praying God will change our prodigal's heart, but also ask God to change our own hearts as well.

The older brother struck out at the father he professed to love and serve and never saw his treatment of his father wasn't any better than the prodigal's. Instead of spending those weeks, months, or even years building up resentment and a sense of entitlement, he would have done better to work on changing himself, developing his character and growing into the best person he could be. And so would we.

If I'm not careful, if you're not careful, we can convince ourselves our prodigal is the only person in our family who has a problem. The truth, however, is our actions and reactions are sometimes as big a problem as anything the prodigal is doing.

Asking God to search our hearts and set a guard on our lips may help relieve the tension in our homes and in our families. We can continue praying God will change our prodigal's heart, but we might also want to ask God to change our own hearts as well.

Something to Think About:

Why is it important to set a guard on our lips? Shouldn't we be able to say what we think?

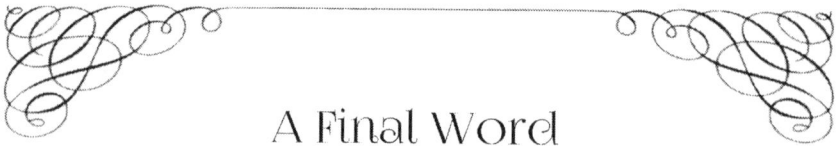

A Final Word

While I can rejoice with the prodigal's father because his son has come home, I wonder whether his homecoming "stuck." Anyone who loves a prodigal knows that isn't certain. We know too well that when our prodigals seem to be doing what's right, it's a gift for today but not a promise for tomorrow.

We've heard their apologies, we've hoped for the best, we've believed they meant it "this time" just to be disappointed again and again. We've entreated the rest of our family like the father entreated the older son, sometimes begging them to show love and forgiveness one to another. And we've tried to be patient, hopeful, and loving like the father. But life doesn't come with guarantees, especially if you love a prodigal.

Those of us who love a prodigal could put our own definition on exhaustion. The people who haven't walked our path can't imagine how weary we become, both physically and emotionally. Now here I am telling you to take your hands off the situation and the broken relationships and "let it go." Letting go is a hard thing to do, isn't it?

I'm not saying it's easy to wait for the prodigal to return or to take our hands off the relationships between the members of our family. It's anything but easy. Being part of a family that loves a prodigal is the most difficult thing I've ever faced.

However, when I stop trying to direct the words and actions of every person in my life and focus instead on making the needed changes in myself, I find reserves of energy I didn't know I had. There is great freedom and even power in recognizing what I can and cannot do and in realizing the only person I can change is myself.

Now we come to the end of the story of the prodigal. But is it really the end? The story leaves me with some unanswered questions. We haven't heard one word from the prodigal since his father restored him to the family. We haven't heard the elder son's answer to the touching entreaty of his father. And we haven't heard the father say the story is over.

It's better this way, don't you think? Life doesn't come neatly packaged with all the results we want and tied with a pretty bow. It's not a destination. It's a journey, and the only part of the journey we have even the smallest control over is our own part. And what is my part? What is yours? What can we do?

I believe we can discipline ourselves to live in hope, and we can continue to do the right thing ourselves in a spirit of hope. We can set limits on the behavior we will tolerate, and we can set boundaries. We can demonstrate our love for the prodigal and the rest of our family by loving them for who they are, what they are, and where they are and waiting for God to make the changes. And we can pray and then take our hands off the situation, leaving the results with a God who loves our prodigal, who loves our family, and who loves us.

PART THREE
Loving a Prodigal Is No Vacation at the Beach

"From the end of the earth will I cry unto thee, when my heart is overwhelmed: lead me to the rock that is higher than I" (Psalm 61:2).

I love the beach. But it's not just the beach. It's everything about vacationing at the beach...the salt water, the sand (yes, even the sand), the sun, the waves and the seafood we eat while we're on vacation. Unfortunately, we don't live close to the ocean. In fact, it's at least five hours to the nearest nirvana, my place of freedom from worry and the external world. With our busy schedules, we don't get to go very often. However, you can be certain we'll see some sand and salt water at least once a year.

Whatever else loving a prodigal might be, it's no vacation at the beach. Matter of fact, it's no vacation at all. It's long, weary days of facing one crisis after another and dark, lonely nights of crying and wondering why our home is in total chaos.

When our loved ones are acting out in destructive ways, we may feel at times like the roof has fallen in, and we are without hope. If you've felt isolated and even abandoned, you're not alone. If you feel like you're the only one trying to do the right thing, you're also not alone. All of us who have ever loved a prodigal have felt the same way sometimes.

Elijah didn't have just a prodigal child or spouse or sister. He had the entire prodigal nation of Israel, whom God had sent him to preach to and minister to. And no matter how many times he showed them God's power, their repentance was short lived. Then they were back into idol worship and every other thing they shouldn't have been doing.

After one of Elijah's greatest victories, the "roof fell in" when Ahab and Jezebel swore they were going to take his life. It was the final straw for God's weary prophet, and, running for his life, he finally became completely discouraged. He didn't have enough hope or energy to even take care of himself.

If you've been walking this path for a while, you can identify with Elijah. It isn't easy to take care of yourself "when the roof falls in," is it? However, God has a plan for you and me and for our lives. In order to fulfill God's purpose and plan, to keep on keeping on instead of quitting when the tough times come, we need to take care of ourselves. After we look at some ways to practice self-care, we'll look at how God ministered to Elijah when His weary, discouraged prophet decided to quit.

On Clouds and Sunshine

Surrounded by the clouds above, dismayed
by heartaches, loss that grieved my soul,
the drops of rain were echoes from a heart,
which in its fragile state did not feel whole.

I longed, as did a king from long ago,
for wings to fly me far away from here
and to a place where peace and rest are found;
but more than that, a respite from my fear.

Then I upon a silver phoenix soared away
and looked amazed at white clouds so reflective.
I had to ask the Lord what made them change.
He answered, "Child, it's only your perspective."

For on the ground, surrounded by the rain,
with vision limited, I see my pain.
But I can know the sun shines way above,
and I can rest in God's unchanging love.

Chapter 7
Whatcha' Gonna' Do When the Roof Falls in?

"For the thing which I greatly feared is come upon me, and that which I was afraid of is come unto me" (Job 3:25).

Have you ever heard the acronym FEAR? It stands for false evidence appearing real. We who love a prodigal often live in the imagined fear of what "might" happen, and most of the things we allow to paralyze us with fear never come to pass. But what about when they do? The phone rings in the middle of the night, the police come to our door, or our prodigal does something so terrible it brings shame, sometimes even public shame, to the family.

Maybe our prodigal ends up paying a terrible price for his or her choices, and maybe the price he or she pays includes prison or even worse. What then? What can we do when a real catastrophe happens and our roof falls in? The following suggestions have worked for many people, and some of them have worked for me.

Allow yourself time to grieve: Whatever caused your roof to fall in, it was a loss for you, and grief is our natural response to a loss. Without listing or discussing all the stages of grief, which start with denial and end with acceptance, I'll only say it can be a long, agonizing path from that denial to acceptance. And it takes time. Those of us who have suffered a profound loss need time to process our loss before healing can even begin to take place.

We need to give ourselves permission to take the time we need and to feel what we feel without beating ourselves up or questioning our spirituality. When our world is in shambles, our heart is in shreds, and our situation appears hopeless, it isn't the time to rebuke ourselves or let others rebuke us for our "lack of faith." Only someone who has never walked the hard path you and I are walking would tell you, "it's time to move on." Allow yourself time to grieve.

Now the worst thing you can imagine has happened, and you're overwhelmed with a flood of emotions: anger, fear, betrayal, and hopelessness, to name a few. Do any of those words describe what you're feeling? The answer is you're probably feeling all those emotions and many more.

I've already said we need to allow ourselves some time to grieve. I didn't put a time limit on it, because the length of time can vary with the individual and the circumstances. And right now you may be thinking you'll never see an end to it. So we grieve. Then what?

Reach out for help and support: Regardless of how terrible our circumstances are, a burden shared is only half as heavy as it will be if you or I try to carry it alone. If drugs or alcohol play a part in the crisis and you don't already go to an Alanon support group, find one and take your heartache there. Those folks will empathize and share with you from their own experience, strength, and hope.

You'll come to realize those people understand you and your pain the same way one wounded soldier understands another wounded soldier's pain. They will help you face the most heart-rending tragedies with poise and dignity and will carry you and your heartache close to themselves. Best of all, you can trust them to respect your privacy.

Alanon isn't the only option for reaching out. You might want to consider going to your pastor or priest, Sunday School teacher, or a trusted friend. I want to add a word of caution here. Be careful about choosing the person or persons you are going to trust with your broken heart. The person you confide in should be someone whose discretion and sensitivity you're confident you can rely on.

To put it bluntly, you don't want to confide in someone who is going to broadcast your personal hurt to the world at large or even to one other person. Be careful about the people with whom you share, but reach out to someone.

I've seen miracles happen when a small group agreed to pray together about a situation or a person. So don't automatically reject the idea of reaching out to a small (emphasis *small*) group. But keep in mind there is nothing to be gained from taking a microphone and announcing from the pulpit at church or posting on social media what's going on in your life or in the life of your prodigal.

Some things you're facing might be too big or too overwhelming for any of the suggestions listed above. Or it might be you have been doing this for so long you're too exhausted to even take some emotional baby steps.

If that's where you find yourself, don't be afraid to seek out professional counseling. The cost may be less than you think, and some therapists offer counseling with the cost on a sliding scale or even free. Some Alanon groups exist under the umbrella of the hospital chaplain's office, and the chaplain will sometimes offer individual counseling. Some churches offer counseling, either pastoral or professional (or both).

Whatever option or options you choose, you should know you are not alone. Many others have walked the same path before you, including me, and we will understand your pain. You don't have to walk this terrible path by yourself.

I saved the most important and most available option for help until last. You can take it to God. If you're angry, even at Him, you can say so. God is bigger than our problems, and He is greater than our anger. And He experienced pain as none have before or after Him. Ask Him to give you comfort and to lead you to someone who will understand your pain, someone who will comfort and encourage you on the path you have to walk. Only God can turn a tragedy into a blessing, but He can if you'll let him. Oh yes, He can!

We've allowed ourselves time to grieve and reach out to others and to God. But how are we supposed to carry on, putting one foot in front of the other day after day when our whole world has crashed around us? When we have been battered and wounded, suffering agonies of soul beyond our ability to express, what then? What are we to do?

Do what you would normally do: You may be thinking that is the dumbest, most insensitive suggestion you've ever heard and maybe you're right. But let me share a story I heard a long time ago that expressed this much better than I could.

In a Scottish mining town, a woman named Molly was sitting in her living room one afternoon when through her window she saw the pastor of her little church walking up the road toward her house. Women in a mining town live with some level of fear all the time, and she knew the pastor wouldn't come visiting in the middle of the afternoon unless it was to bring tragic news. It was with a pounding heart she met him at the door, and she knew from his face the news he was bringing her was the worst possible. Sure enough, the preacher told Molly her husband had been killed in a cave in.

Molly sat quietly for a few minutes. Then she stood up and went into the kitchen and put a kettle on for tea. The preacher watched her in amazement and finally asked, "Molly, did you not hear me tell you the terrible thing that happened?" Molly answered she had indeed heard him. "Then what are you doing?" he asked.

Molly, with stricken eyes and tears streaming down her face replied, "I'm doing what I would be doing if this terrible thing had not happened." Molly's answer didn't mean her grief wasn't real. It was real, and it was evident from the pain in her face and from her tears. So I'll second the preacher's question, What in the world was she doing?

Molly knew she could find comfort, however small, in doing the routine things she always did. What worked for her will work for us. When we are still reeling from our roof falling in, and we don't know what to do next, we can bring a little order into our chaos by doing what we would normally do. It may mean playing the piano, going for a walk, taking a shower, or making a pot of tea. Easier said than done? You bet. But if we can discipline ourselves to get up and do the next right thing, it will bring some measure of normalcy to a world that has become temporarily insane. And I do mean temporarily. This isn't going to last forever, no matter how much it seems that way right now.

Grieving, reaching out, and doing the next right thing are all tools, which are available to us when our "roof falls in." But you've done those things and continue to do them, and it seems like this has gone on forever. You see no resolution, and you're exhausted. Sure you are, and so are all the others I've known who have walked a path like ours, including me—at least sometimes. What then? I can best answer that by looking at the experience of someone who was as overwhelmed as we sometimes are.

That someone would be the prophet Elijah. I love the story in 1 Kings 18 of Elijah and the prophets of Baal. You've got to love it when the good guys win, don't you? And did he ever! First he faced King Ahab down. Then he stood alone against 450 prophets of Baal, and God showed Himself powerful on behalf of Elijah and gave him the greatest victory of his ministry. Then what?

1 Kings 19 is another story about Elijah—one of fear, exhaustion, and discouragement. Did this powerful man of God experience total defeat immediately after a total victory? Yes. Some may wonder how he could be completely discouraged after seeing God work, but those of us who have walked a hard path day after day because of a prodigal understand it completely.

A great victory for God didn't change the fact that Elijah had a broken heart. My heart hurts for Elijah, who was sitting under the juniper tree, completely defeated. I can't help but identify with him when he told God, "It is enough; now, O Lord, take away my life." He was finished—at least for the moment.

We can learn some things from how God ministered to Elijah in his sad and lonely wilderness. God's tender care of his prophet can show us how to take care of ourselves when our own situation seems overwhelming or hopeless—when we are in our own wilderness of the soul.

Before we look at how God used one of His angels to show Elijah some things he needed to do to take care of himself, we'll take a look at where Elijah was, both physically and emotionally. I didn't add spiritually because I believe the spiritual part is going to be difficult, if not impossible, if the other two things aren't taken care of. So who was Elijah, and why was he at the end of himself?

Elijah's ministry as a prophet was almost entirely about confronting sin among the leaders first and then all Israel as well and warning them of the coming judgment of God. Most of the miracles he did had to do with that judgment. Not the kind of job to foster positive thinking, and he had been doing it for several years. I can see how he would be emotionally exhausted.

Also, he had made quite a journey after confronting Ahab and the prophets of Baal. He walked or ran about 30 miles to escape from Ahab and another 60 miles running from Jezebel. Running for your life qualifies as having the roof fall in, doesn't it? At this point in his life, Elijah was as stressed and desperate as any of us. And it wasn't because he was unspiritual. Elijah was very spiritual, but he was also exhausted.

After walking or running for 90 miles, he left his servant and went yet another "day's journey" into the wilderness. A day's journey added about another 15 miles for a total of more than a hundred miles, and he was far from being a young man. It's not hard to understand why he was sleeping under the juniper tree.

Like those of us who love a prodigal, Elijah had a difficult path to walk. No wonder he told God, "It is enough." He was finished, or at least he thought he was. This wasn't a brief walk in the desert to look at the flowers. In his exhaustion and discouragement, Elijah had plans for a permanent vacation. He was done.

That's when God sent an angel to minister to Elijah and to give him the things he was going to need for his journey. In reading about what Elijah needed, I learned some things, which have helped me through some tough times. Maybe some of those things will help you as well. What were Elijah needs, and how did God meet those needs?

Something to Think About:

Why do you think it's important to reach out for support when your world is upside down and your family is in crisis?

Chapter 8
Elijah's Vacation in the Wilderness

"Whither shall I go from thy spirit? or whither shall I flee from thy presence…thou art there" (Psalm 139:7-8).

If you're going on vacation, you will need several things. And although Elijah's time in the wilderness was hardly a vacation, he was going to need some things as well. You don't take time to pack two or three bags to take along if you're running from a king and queen who intend to kill you. So Elijah had some basic physical needs. However, he also had some other needs. And they were the kind of needs only God could meet.

He needed to know he wasn't alone: Elijah thought he was alone. "And I, even I alone, am left" (1 Kings 19:11). It wasn't the first time Elijah had felt defeated and alone. He used almost those same words in 1 Kings 18 when he was facing the 450 prophets of Baal. He thought he was the only person left who loved the Lord, and his weary heart was broken.

The loneliness of a broken heart is a terrible thing, and the temptation for us is to go even further into the empty wilderness of isolation just as Elijah did. But Elijah was wrong. He wasn't the only one left who wanted to do the right thing. He wasn't alone, and neither are we. In his discouragement, he couldn't see the whole picture. Nor can you and I when our hearts are in shreds, and tears blur our vision.

He needed to sleep: Simplistic? Yes, but true nonetheless. For those of us who love a prodigal, sleep is not always a given. But I don't need to tell you that. We've experienced the middle of the night phone calls and text messages, the "emergencies," which could have waited until morning, and the stress. Oh, and the heartache that robs us of our sleep. Shame, regret and guilt we don't deserve can also keep us awake. And the fear—let's not forget the fear. What can we do?

I've started leaving my cell phone in the living room at night. A friend downloaded a "silent" ring for her iPhone and assigned it to her prodigal. Her reasoning? She knows if he calls, but only if she checks her phone. She doesn't attempt to stop his frequent and sometimes abusive calls or to control him in any way. However, the silent ring tone means she deals with his phone calls or with him when she's ready. She said, "If it were a true emergency and I was needed, someone else would let me know." And she's right.

Others have told me they took a warm bath, listened to soothing music, and gave their prodigal to God in prayer before going to bed. One friend said she pictures herself wrapping her prodigal in a blanket and handing him over to God and saying, "Here he is, God. You take care of him so I can sleep." What a concept! Another friend told me she says the Serenity Prayer over and over again until she falls asleep.

Some of those suggestions may work for you. Whatever you have to do to make it happen, you need to sleep. I'll add a word of caution here. It's not a good idea to use alcohol or medications like Xanax or Valium to help you sleep. It's possible, even likely, those things will cause more problems than you already have.

He needed to eat and drink: Again, this is pretty simple, but it's just as necessary. How does it profit our prodigal or anyone else if we don't eat? We're going to have times when stress takes away our appetite, and I understand that. But who says we need to have an appetite in order to eat? We can choose to eat because our bodies need fuel, and it's the responsible thing to do.

I don't need to be a martyr today, and neither do you. Giving our body the nourishment it

The loneliness of a broken heart is a terrible thing.

needs is a choice we can make regardless of how we feel. If God thought Elijah needed food and drink, don't you think we need it too? And doing these simple things to take care of ourselves can help us regain some control, at least in some small parts of our lives.

You would think Elijah, with his own private angel to minister to and serve him, would have regained his strength and courage. But it didn't work out that way, and Elijah found some things he couldn't do.

He couldn't see God's gentle hand: Elijah ate the food prepared by an angel, and he was so exhausted he went back to sleep. I don't want to just rush past this without thinking about it for a minute. He didn't stop at McDonald's, and it wasn't a pizza delivered by Papa John's. We're talking about an *angel*, who had been sent by God to minister directly, one-on-one, to Elijah!

And in spite of his own private miracle and in the presence of an angel, he ate and went back to sleep? He didn't even say, "Wow?" Hard to believe, but are we really any different? I am sometimes so overwhelmed and bewildered by the circumstances around me, I can't see or appreciate how God is working, and I often can't see His hand or feel His gentle touch. I sometimes waste so much energy grieving the things I think are forever lost, I can't rejoice in the things which remain. And that's where Elijah was.

He couldn't pray: After Elijah told God he wanted to die, we don't hear another word from him while he was under the juniper tree. He was finished; at least he thought he was. The time would come when he would have another conversation with God, but it wasn't going to happen in the middle of the wilderness. At this point, he was too discouraged to do anything for anyone, even himself.

A long time ago, someone told me the day would come when life had battered me so much I wouldn't be able to pray. He also told me when that day came, I shouldn't worry about it if people rebuked me for my "lack of faith."

Those times did come and still sometimes do, but God knows what you and I need without our having to ask. And He's in the middle of our storms, whether we can feel His presence or not. In those moments, it may be all we can do to sit there, helpless and broken, and wait for God to send an angel. The good news is it's ok if you're there sometimes. You aren't always going to feel that way, and you will eventually come out on the other side of the hard time you're facing right now. Until then, if you're sometimes too overwhelmed to pray, you can rest in the assurance that God knows and understands.

He couldn't find strength to go on: The angel woke Elijah a second time and told him he needed to eat again. The angel didn't give Elijah a pep-talk or tell him about the "power of positive thinking." He didn't tell him to read a book about being an overcomer, to write about it, to "look on the bright side," or to stop complaining about it. The angel didn't even ask Elijah what he thought about it. He just told Elijah what the weary prophet already knew, "the journey is too great for you" (1 Kings 19:7).

If you're reading this, you've no doubt spent some time in that kind of wilderness. You may even be in a wilderness now. And I'm not going to try to tell you everything is going to come out "happy, happy, joy, joy" because sometimes it doesn't. However, it's important to note the next word in those verses is "went." Quitting wasn't an option for Elijah, and it's not an option for us either.

Elijah's journey wasn't over. He had to continue on the path before him whether he wanted to or not. But he didn't go in his own strength because he couldn't. He had none. He also didn't ask God to give him strength because he couldn't even pray, at least not at the moment. But he was able to get up and start putting one foot in front of the other in the strength God gave him. Elijah's story wasn't even close to being finished yet. Neither is your story or mine.

I'm reminded of a friend, who lost her only son. Her son was not a prodigal, but that didn't make her loss any greater or any less. Like Elijah, she was devastated by her circumstances, isolated by her loss, and without hope for the future. She felt totally alone. At one point, she asked God, "Where are you? You promised You would never leave me or forsake me. But I'm alone, my son is gone, and You aren't here for me!"

My friend said God touched her broken heart and whispered, "Who do you think gives you the strength to get out of bed each day?" Her pain and loss were so great she couldn't even begin to express it to anyone or ask for help. The journey was too much for her.

She was a grieving mother, who didn't have the strength in herself to get out of bed. And even with God's help, it was a major accomplishment just to do such a small thing. Like Elijah, all she could do in the middle of her wilderness was to keep putting one foot in front of the other.

Like my friend, I've been in the wilderness too, without strength, without courage, without hope. But my friend's story wasn't finished yet; it still isn't finished as God continues to do a work in her life. And your story and mine? They aren't finished yet either.

It's hard to see God's hand working when our hearts are breaking, isn't it? And it's hard to exercise faith when we're devastated by loss. For today, maybe it's enough just to draw on God's strength to get out of bed and then to remember we don't have to run a marathon today.

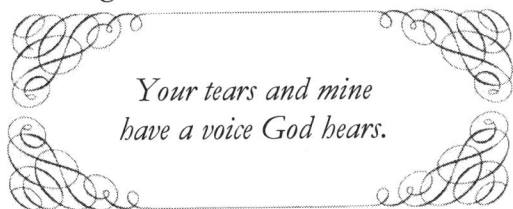

Your tears and mine have a voice God hears.

And if we don't have the emotional energy to talk about our prodigals or our losses or to reach out or even to pray, it's ok. Your tears and mine have a voice God hears (Psalm 6:8), and if tears are all you have on a given day, it's enough. How's this for a thought? Be gentle with yourself today. It could be the journey is too much for you.

He couldn't see God's purpose: Elijah's journey in the wilderness wasn't without purpose. He had a destination. Through the food and drink the angel gave Elijah, God gave him the strength to walk to Mount Horeb, which is another name for Mount Sinai, also called the "mountain of God."

Mount Sinai is synonymous with holiness. It was where God told Moses to take his shoes off because he was standing on holy ground. It was where God gave Moses the Ten Commandments. It was a place where God met with His people and did great things. Now God was going to meet Elijah on His holy mountain as well.

I'm comforted when I realize I can go to God with things that are overwhelming to me. And I can be sure He will not only meet me when I go to Him, but He will also give me the strength and desire to go to Him in the first place. I'm not talking about church, although an old-fashioned altar is a great place to go with my pain, ask God to take it, and leave it with Him—at least for a little while.

I'm talking about those midnight hours when we don't know where our prodigals are, don't know what they're doing or whether they are safe, and we can't see any hope of change. If you're like me, you've faced those midnight hours with fear, discouragement, and a broken heart.

In our joy when our prayers have been answered, and our prodigals have returned, God will be with us. But He is also present in the midnight hours and in the darkness of despair, when we can't see any hope, and when we can't understand or see God's purpose. God is still sovereign, He is still faithful, and He is still with us even in the darkest midnight.

For someone who had seen God do great things, had spoken directly to God and received direct answers, and had been cared for by an angel, Elijah was clueless about some things. He thought God was finished with him. He was wrong. He thought he could quit his ministry. He was wrong. He thought he was the only one left doing the right thing. Again, he was wrong. He thought he could hide out in a cave for the rest of his life. Oh, but he was wrong.

He couldn't hear God in the storm: When God asked Elijah why he was in the cave, Elijah answered with the same discouragement as before. Can you understand and identify with his discouragement? Although the Israelites had made a show of repentance, Elijah knew it wouldn't last. They had disappointed him again and again. And when disappointments follow the times of momentary hope, those disappointments are the most bitter of all.

God revealed Himself to Elijah in a most unusual way. At first, God sent a great wind, an earthquake, and a fire. All those are very dramatic and powerful things, which are associated with catastrophe. But that isn't what God wanted Elijah to see about Him. After they had all passed, God was still present and speaking in a "still small voice" (1 Kings 9:11-12).

The thing about a "still small voice" is that I need to be quiet and still myself in order to hear it. Being quiet and still is hard to do when storms are raging, the wind is blowing, and our hearts are overwhelmed. Elijah couldn't hear God's "still small voice" in the midst of the wind, the earthquake or the fire either. But in the quiet, when those things had passed, he could hear God's gentle voice, which had been speaking to him all the time.

God isn't going to abandon us in our midnight hours. He's too faithful to do such a thing. If we can't see or hear Him, it's because our storms are fierce, and our faith is small. However, if we let Him, He can quiet my heart and yours, soothe our fears and help us to know He is with us in a "still small voice."

When God spoke to him, Elijah covered his face with his mantle, a sign of respect and an acknowledgment of the sovereignty of God. Then he went and stood at the entrance to the cave. When God asked him again why he was there, Elijah's answer was the same. What? Had Elijah learned nothing? On the surface, it would seem so. But a closer look at the Scriptures tells a different story.

1 Kings 19:9 tells us Elijah came and *lodged* in the cave. I mean he moved in with all his bags and set up housekeeping. He put his recliner in a convenient spot, his big screen TV in the corner, his favorite picture on the wall. His full intent was to stay in that cave forever. He was finished.

The fireworks of the earthquake, the mighty wind, and the fire got his attention, and he listened when God spoke to him. Did he go back to the cave? Oh, yes. But we find him standing at the *entrance* of the cave. He wasn't unpacking his bags, sitting in the recliner watching an Alabama football game, or hiding in the closet. He wasn't all the way on the victory side, but he wasn't setting up housekeeping in the cave any more either.

The fresh smell of nature, which is obvious after the storm is over isn't even noticeable in the middle of the storm. We don't think about how the rain is feeding the parched earth when we're in the midst of the thunder and lightning. But our limited vision doesn't make it less true. Learning to trust God in the storm was a process for Elijah, perhaps a life-long process. It will be a process for us too, and we won't always feel like we're making progress.

It was my privilege some time ago to hear a friend speak about her battle with leukemia and what her journey had been like. Before her illness, she had been the director of the Ladies Ministry at her church.

I expected to hear her say she had trusted God through her illness and had felt His presence every day in her wilderness journey. I thought she would say God is powerful and had performed a miracle in her recovery because I knew both those things were true.

I thought she would say God had caused her faith to grow, but that wasn't her story at all. She talked about being afraid, about feeling isolated, about being so weak and battered from the leukemia and the chemo, she couldn't even pray. And then she said she's still not "all the way back" to where she was, physically, emotionally and yes, even spiritually.

Wow! Were those words from someone for whom God had performed a miracle, one of the leaders in her Ladies' Ministry, and one of my personal heroes? Yes, and yes, and yes. Why? Because when your roof falls in, recovery is a process and not an event. Healing takes time, and we need to be patient with the process and patient with ourselves during the process.

I don't know what burdens you're carrying today. Whatever they are, burdens almost always involve a loss. It might be the loss of a loved one through death, separation or divorce or the loss of a relationship or because your prodigal is in "a far country." Whatever the loss and whatever your burden, when your roof falls in, repairing the roof won't happen in five minutes, five hours, or five days. It may take a lifetime.

I'm thankful for my friend's honesty. Because when we're authentic, it gives others permission to be open and honest as well. Her story reminded me God "knows our frame and remembers we are dust" (Psalm 103:14). It means I don't have to be a giant in my faith. I just need to be real, keep taking those baby steps, and wait for God to work. God wasn't through with Elijah, he isn't through with my friend, and He isn't through with you and me.

Something to Think About:

What are some ways you can be gentle with yourself during your storm?

PART FOUR

What You Can't Do, What You Can Do, Why You Can't Quit

> "And let us not be weary in well doing: for in due season we shall reap, if we faint not" (Galatians 6:9).

When I spoke to a support group called "Parents of Prodigals" in Marietta, Georgia, the raw pain in that room was almost a tangible, living thing. Most of those parents had kids who had just begun to act out, and the parents were stunned and hurting. If there's anything more bewildering, frightening or overwhelming than having a prodigal wreak havoc in your home, I don't know what it could be.

Like you, like me, those parents had hopes and dreams for their kids. They cared for them when they were babies, invested in their lives as they started school or played sports, and may even have prayed for them every day of their lives. Now their kids were out of control, the parents' hearts were broken, and they didn't know what to do.

Loving a prodigal is hard, whether it's your teenager, adult child, spouse or another loved one. The hardest part is the total helplessness we feel when our world is falling apart. Realizing we are powerless to "fix" our loved one or to stop the insanity in our family may be the most frightening thing in the world. And if you're ready to throw up your hands and quit, who could blame you?

I can't tell you how to "fix" anyone or anything, but I've learned (usually the hard way) some specific things those of us who love a prodigal can and can't do. As we begin to recognize and then accept those things we can't change, it leaves us free to focus on the things we can. There are many things we can do as assuredly as there are some we can't.

As we busy ourselves with the things we can change, we'll learn little by little to accept the things we can't. A big part of accepting the things I can't change is reminding myself "God's got this." He really does, you know, and that's the reason I won't quit until God answers my prayers and brings my prodigal back home.

Let It Go

Some people with a problem
are quite a sight to see.
I'm filled with real amazement
and some perplexity.
When faced with a dilemma,
they say they just don't know.
But when God tries to take it,
they simply won't let go.

They lay it at the altar
of God in prayer and then
when they get up to walk away,
they pick it up again.
They pray in desperation
when they've done all they can.
Then they want the Lord to work
according to their plan.

I admit that I'm confused.
It makes no sense to me
that we hold on to worry
when God would set us free.
We can't choose God's agenda
for we don't know His plan.
And don't you think that some things
are best not left to man?

Trust Him to know the answers
and do what He thinks best.
You just do what you can do
and leave Him with the rest.
Precious, troubled child of God,
I think you need to know:
To let this be God's problem,
you'll have to let it go.

Chapter 9
What You Can't Do

You can't keep lying to yourself: I've heard this kind of denial compared to having an elephant in the living room. Everyone walks around it, avoiding it if they can and occasionally bumping into it. We dust it and polish it; we might even put a tablecloth or a lamp on it. The only thing we don't do is say, "Hey! There's an elephant in the living room!"

While the elephant story may be amusing, lying to ourselves about the problems in our home isn't amusing at all. I continue to be astounded at the capacity we all have for self-deception, especially where our families are concerned. Everything in our child's life is screaming he is in trouble—failing grades, breaking curfew. Maybe he was suspended from school.

We may have found beer cans in his car or marijuana in his dresser, and we wanted to believe him when he said it "belonged to a friend." Did we worry he was hanging out with the "wrong crowd?" If our child is an adult, his marriage might be breaking up or he may have been arrested for a DUI. If it's our spouse, do we pretend we don't see the amount of alcohol he's drinking or know how many nights he doesn't come home?

Dysfunction and substance abuse thrive in the dark. Not only will denial not cause the problem to go away, it will actually cause it to grow and become worse. The first step in problem solving is to recognize and admit there is a problem.

97

You can't "fix" your prodigal: What? You just told me I needed to recognize there's a problem, and now you're telling me I can't fix it? Living with a prodigal, whether we recognize it or not, has conditioned us to think we can fix anything. I mean, after all, we're the ones who have kept the home functioning, aren't we? Well, sort of. And we're the ones who have paid the bills, called the bosses, intervened with the courts and gone to the schools.

But if we're honest with ourselves, we'll see those have been Band-Aid fixes at best. They didn't really fix anything at all. How could they? "Fixing" our prodigals would mean we're able to control the minds, hearts, and behavior of another human being. Besides, what we want isn't just for them to do the right thing, is it? We want them to *want* to do the right thing. However, the decision to do what's right is theirs alone and out of our control, and so is their behavior.

You can't "fix" the relationships: When someone is doing destructive things and creating chaos in a family, that person's relationships are certain to suffer. It's not our responsibility to fix them. Good thing, too, because we can't. If we can't "fix" our own relationship with our prodigal, how can we hope to fix his relationships with anyone else?

I know it hurts to see the broken relationships in our family, and I know how much we wish we could do something to heal them. However, it's one of the many things beyond our control. So we have to step back and let the people we love figure out those relationships for themselves. We also need to recognize some of those relationships won't be healed until our prodigal "comes to himself" and is willing to do what's right.

Three things stand out when we consider the problem of our prodigals and their relationships. 1) We can't "fix" the damage they have done to relationships or repair the wrongs they have done. And why would we think it's our place to do that? 2) We can't erase the scars, resentment or bitterness resulting from months and sometimes years of abuse or make anyone forgive them. Not my job. Not yours. 3) We can't control what other people think or say about our prodigal.

You can't control what people say: People can be cruel, can't they? You would think your family, your friends and your church would support you when your heart is broken over a prodigal. But sometimes it doesn't work that way. Your son has been arrested or your daughter has told you she's pregnant. You see true repentance, and your prodigal chose to be honest. In the case of the daughter, she chose to do the more difficult thing by having the baby instead of getting an abortion.

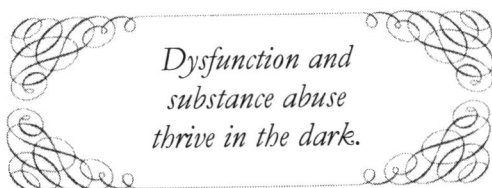

Dysfunction and substance abuse thrive in the dark.

Instead of receiving compassion from your church family and your friends, the people in your family (and perhaps you) are treated with contempt. They (and perhaps you) might even be the subject of gossip, thinly veiled as "prayer requests." In any of those situations, we can't control what people think or what they say. What's the answer?

We were never meant to find our help in men, but in God (Psalm 146:3). Does it hurt? Of course, it does. We're only human. So we also need to guard our hearts against bitterness. And if people have a problem with our prodigal, with our family or with us, we need to let it be their problem because it *is* their problem. If you love a prodigal, you have enough problems of your own without taking on anyone else's problems.

You can't force your desired outcome: And that's true, regardless of what your desired outcome might be or even how right or noble it might be. Many years ago, I belonged to a church that had a bus ministry. A little guy named Billy rode the bus to church with his little sister, Susie. He was eight or nine and went into the regular service, but she was about four so she was in Junior Church.

During the invitation at the end of the service every Sunday, Billy would go get little Susie from Junior Church and drag her to the altar in the auditorium. She would be protesting (loudly), "I don't wanna' go, I don't wanna' go!" And he would be responding (loudly), "You're going!"

What a sight the two of them were! The church couldn't help but be amused. We were touched as well by how much he loved and worried about his little sister. She, of course, didn't understand and wasn't ready to make any decision for Christ. One of the counselors would pray with both kids and tell Billy, "She's not ready yet—we'll just pray for her."

While we may be smiling and shaking our heads at Billy's actions, haven't we done some things just as silly? We've gone through our prodigals' phones to see what numbers they have called and made sure we knew every person associated with those numbers. We've read their text messages and even put taps on our home phones.

We've found them jobs and made out the applications, we've signed them up for classes or training, and we've asked people to "have a talk with them." We've even invited the preacher or someone else to drop in and "surprise" us (and them) with a visit.

The problem with doing those things is we can't force or trick someone into doing the right thing or into making a decision for Christ, no matter how pure our motivation. It hasn't worked for you so far, has it? And the definition of insanity is, "Doing the same things over and over again, expecting different results."

Those are a few of the things from a long list of what we can't do. There are, however, some things we can do. Knowing what they are and practicing them will help us retain some sanity when our lives are in chaos.

Something to Think About:

Have you tried "fixing" your prodigal or his damaged relationships with others? What was the result?

Chapter 10
What You Can Do

You can stop blaming yourself: Have you made mistakes in raising your children? Join the club. So have we all. I've already discussed at length parental versus personal responsibility so I won't rehash it again. I will only say we did the best we could with what we had at the time, like every other parent in the world. You and I couldn't give what we did not have. If you know you've made mistakes, and we all have, confess them, forgive yourself and move on. Bottom line? Your prodigal acting out isn't payback for something you did or didn't do.

You can stop blaming others: Just as the choices your prodigal makes aren't your fault, they also aren't the fault of your spouse, your other kids, your prodigal's friends, his teachers, or your pastor. Your son or daughter isn't acting out because of an absent father or the youth pastor who hurt his or her feelings.

It's also not the fault of the "wrong crowd." Some parents have tried putting their kids in a different school or even moving to another town. However, it only took their kids about a week to find another "wrong crowd." I can't tell you the number of times young people, who were in treatment or in a half-way house, have told me their parents thought their problem was hanging out with the "wrong crowd," when in reality they themselves were the wrong crowd.

Nobody is responsible for the actions of your prodigal except the prodigal himself. While the "blame game" may make you feel better, it isn't helpful, and it just isn't true.

You can recognize the entire family gets sick: The destructive behavior of a prodigal doesn't happen in a vacuum. He or she may be the only one acting out, but the entire family gets sick. That's a hard concept to understand and accept, but it's true.

When a prodigal is acting out, it creates chaos in the family. The mom has had to be super-responsible, putting on hold any dreams she once had for herself. Whether the prodigal is a spouse or a child, other family members have had to step up to the plate, filling roles they shouldn't have to fill. If the parents are not in agreement about how to deal with the prodigal, it adds another level of pain and confusion to the situation.

Take a look at the word "dysfunction." The prefix "dys" means ill or sick, and implies pain. So you have "sick, painful" functioning. It can also mean "not," and functioning can mean working. So, at best, you have a home situation that is "not working," and the environment is not healthy. How can people not get sick in such a situation or environment?

Some support groups tell you to "live with it or leave." I see the wisdom in those words, but "kicking the bum out" isn't going to solve the entire problem when everyone is sick. What usually happens when the person who is acting out is removed from the scene is that someone else begins to act out. Understanding how all the members of your family are affected will go a long way toward helping you understand why everyone (including you) is acting the way they are.

You can educate yourself: Many resources are available to you if substance abuse is involved. Alanon, Celebrate Recovery, Overcomers Outreach, individual or group counseling, and some small groups at various churches are just a few of the places where you can get information. You can also go to open meetings of Alcoholics Anonymous (AA). Knowledge is power, and you can find hope, help and encouragement from some of these resources. A list of these and other resources is at the end of this book.

You can get help for yourself: While you can't choose recovery for any other person, you can choose to begin a journey of recovery for yourself. Getting back into church would be a good place to start. If your heart is broken and your life is in such chaos that you don't know where to turn, why would you avoid your church? That's the very place where the preaching of God's word could bring comfort, hope and encouragement to your wounded spirit. That's where you can take your heavy burden and leave it with the Lord…at least for a while.

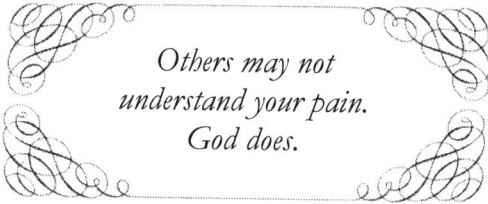

Others may not understand your pain. God does.

Alanon would also be a good place to start. Keep in mind Alanon, Celebrate Recovery and some of these other groups are not going to have a magic wand you can wave over your prodigal and "fix" him or her. What they can do is encourage you and help you to work on yourself and your own recovery.

You can continue to do the right thing: Not as easy as it sounds, is it? As I'm typing this, the names of half a dozen people came to mind. They were hurt by the actions of a prodigal and have dropped out of everything that once mattered to them.

I understand the embarrassment and "borrowed shame" associated with loving a prodigal. And I've experienced some of the struggles you are facing now. I know what it feels like to have the husband walk away. I've wept over a child I love, who acted out and broke my heart. And I know how public embarrassment and humiliation can go along with those things. I've been there.

However, staying away from church, dropping out of the choir or giving up your Sunday School class isn't going to help you face an impossible situation. And none of those is doing the right thing. Turning your back on your church isn't going to help your family or your prodigal. Nor is it in your best interest. I can speak from personal experience and tell you walking away from God will take you places you'll wish someday you hadn't gone.

Now is the time to cling more closely to your family, your friends, your faith. The time is going to come when you and the people you care about are going to come out on the other side of your broken hearts, and you're going to look back on these hard days in the wilderness. Let it not be said of you that you stopped doing what you knew was right because someone hurt you.

You can stop "rescuing" your prodigal: I could pitch a tent here and camp for a while. Why? Because it seems so obvious it's not the thing to do, but all of us who love a prodigal have done it, and some of us continue to do it…to our prodigal's detriment and our own.

I was teaching a class for the Court Referral Program, and every student in the class had been arrested for either a drug or an alcohol offence. An elderly lady walked into the classroom because she thought it was the place to bail her son out of jail. She shared how it had taken her three or four days to put together the money, and she had sold some things to do it. The sorrow and worry on her face were heart wrenching. One little old lady did more to speak to my students in three minutes than I could have in a month.

I told her where she needed to go and, as she was leaving, I said, "Ma'am?" When she turned, I asked, "Why don't you go home, make yourself a cup of tea, and just leave your son where he is?" When she said she couldn't leave him in jail, I asked the class how many of them thought that's what she should do. Every one of my 18 students raised their hands. And they are the ones who would know.

If you and I are shielding our prodigals from the logical consequences of their choices, we are not helping them. We're hurting them. Had the father of the prodigal in the parable been rescuing his son every time things went wrong, his prodigal son never would have "come to himself" in the pigsty.

If we keep getting in the way when God is trying to get our prodigal's attention, we shouldn't wonder if things don't change. Maybe it's time for us to step back, mind our own business and let the prodigal figure things out for himself.

You can pray: People may stop here and say, "Well, of course! I know that!" You may even be rolling your eyes. But think about it for a minute. The great God who spoke, and the universe came to be, the God who breathes out suns and galaxies—He will incline His ear to hear you. To hear me. This God is the One who knows your name, sees every tear you've shed and hears your every broken-hearted prayer. Others may not understand your pain. God does.

Friends may walk away as though your pain and sorrow were contagious. Jesus will never forsake you. And regardless of how awful your situation is, the God who loves you with an everlasting love is going to work your heartache out somehow for your good (Romans 8:28). Because of His faithfulness, we can have courage. Because of His goodness, we can have hope. And because of His tender love for us, we can pray.

You can choose to forgive: Ouch! That's a hard one, isn't it? Forgiveness means giving up your right to strike back and hurt someone who has hurt you. Seeing forgiveness as a choice instead of a feeling and then doing it aren't easy when you love a prodigal. But I can't tell you how important it is for us to do both those things.

In fact, forgiveness is such an important part of the entire picture, I've devoted an entire section of this book to it. So I won't spend a lot of time focusing on it here. I'll only say if you love a prodigal, you're going to have a lot of opportunities to practice forgiveness and not just with your prodigal.

You can refuse to quit: Refusing to quit regardless of what happens may be the most challenging thing on the list of things you can do. I know how hard it is to love a prodigal. I'm walking the same path you are. I also know how often our choices are limited and how often those choices are impacted by others. However, the choice to keep on keeping on is ours alone.

If you have never been tempted to give up on your prodigal, your family, your church, yourself and even your God, you're made of stronger stuff than most of us. You're made of stronger stuff than I. How can we not become discouraged when each day brings new pain, when we've cried until we have no more tears and when our prayers seem to be in vain?

Loving a prodigal means living a life of ongoing losses, forgiving only to be hurt over and over again. And you may have been doing it for a long time. If you're weary, discouraged and tempted to quit, I don't blame you. I've been there too; sometimes I'm still there.

Recognizing what we can do and what we can't do isn't easy. Applying the knowledge by letting go of the things we can't change and being courageous enough to change the things we can is even more difficult. Lasting change takes time and effort, but we can make a beginning. And even the smallest baby steps will help us take back control of our lives a little bit at a time.

Something to Think About:

In what ways has your family changed since your prodigal began to act out?

Chapter 11
Why You Can't Quit

If you're like me or like the hundreds of people who have shared the story of their journey with me, you have sometimes wanted to quit. You may even be facing one of those times right now. If you are, it's not surprising because when you love a prodigal, the path you walk each day is not an easy one. At times, it can be brutal, and it's easy to feel discouraged.

I have yet to hear from someone who loves a prodigal who hasn't felt discouraged at times. Days can stretch into weeks and months and sometimes years without our prodigals showing any inclination of coming home. It's understandable if you sometimes ask, "How long, Lord?"

When each day brings new hurt and disappointment, when it seems like our prayers don't go higher than the ceiling, when we begin to wonder if God even cares how we are hurting, we may feel like quitting. Who wouldn't? While our reasons for wanting to quit are valid, there are also valid reasons why we can't quit. I've listed a few of them.

Because we can hope in God: "Why art thou cast down, O my soul? and why art thou disquieted within me? Hope thou in God" (Psalm 42:5, 11).

I love the Psalms. I find great comfort in reading about King David's fears and sorrows. My heart is encouraged when I read how he lifted up his voice to God and found in Him a haven of rest for his soul. In the midst of his greatest sorrow,

David reached out to God and trusted He would meet the need of his heart. And God did.

In Psalm 42, David says his tears seemed to say to him, "Where is your God?" Can you identify with him? I know I can. When the people I love are hurting themselves, each other, and me, I sometimes have to ask myself where God is.

Doesn't He see how much I'm hurting? Doesn't He know my prodigal is destroying the lives of everyone around him? Doesn't He care my grandchildren are suffering and my heart is broken for those little ones? How can I find hope in my own midnight of the soul?

David found hope in remembering. He remembered going to the house of God and taking others with him. He remembered better times, times of joy and thanksgiving. He remembered being a spiritual leader. He remembered other times he had faced troubles and how God had been faithful every time. He remembered, and so can you and I.

I'm not at the point where I can "glory in tribulations" (Romans 5:8), but I can and I do remember God was faithful every time I had a problem, even if I couldn't see it at the time. I can remember how those problems taught me patience and how to wait for God's timing. They also gave me experience both in facing trials and in turning them over to God. The experience I've gained is what gives me hope today, hope in the unchanging God, who won't leave me ashamed or disappointed.

While it's true "hope deferred makes the heart sick," it's also true that "when the desire comes..." Oh, when it comes! When God shows Himself powerful on my behalf, on yours, "it is a tree of life" (Proverbs 13:12). Knowing God hears and answers prayer is why I can say with the Psalmist, "Why art thou cast down, oh my soul? and why art thou disquieted within me? Hope thou in God" (Psalm 43:5).

Until that day comes, you and I can you remind ourselves of times in the past when God met our needs. Can you remember times when things looked hopeless, but God showed up just in time? Of course, you can. And so can I. And aren't we trusting Him with our immortal souls?

If you answered yes to those questions, surely you can take your impossible situation and give it to God, trusting Him to show up for you just as He always has in the past. You may have learned to trust Him in the light, but He is just as faithful in the darkness you are facing now. Can you not trust Him in the dark because of what He has proven to you in the light? Knowing we can hope in God is one of the reasons we can't quit.

Because God hasn't quit on you: "Looking unto Jesus the author and finisher of our faith; who for the joy that was set before him endured the cross, despising the shame" (Hebrews 12:2).

I've found I can't rely on my feelings. This is true of most people, but perhaps more true for those of us who love a prodigal. On two separate days, we're likely to feel two separate ways about our circumstances. Often the circumstances haven't changed. In fact, they may have worsened. The only difference is our perspective or mood.

Feelings of sorrow, fear, and even abandonment are going to surface sometimes, but my feelings are unreliable. Because I know how unreliable those feelings are, I have to focus on what I know. And what I know is God has promised He will never leave me, nor will He forsake me. We can't quit or give up on God because He hasn't given up on us.

Have you suffered because of the things your prodigal has done and the choices he has made? Have you asked yourself why you should have to suffer for what someone else has done? Having done nothing wrong Himself, Jesus went to the cross for my sins and yours, and He did it when we were the enemies of God (Colossians 1:21). This verse also tells us He did it "in due time," which means His timing, not ours. Has your prodigal brought you shame? Jesus "endured the cross, despising the shame" (Hebrews 12:12).

In the beginning, Jesus had many disciples following Him. They were hoping He was the Messiah, who would free them from their hated enemies, the Romans. When He told them how it was really going to happen and how difficult the path was going to be, most of them went away. Jesus looked at the 12 who remained and said, "Will ye also go away?" (John 6:67).

In the next verse, Peter replied, "To whom shall we go?" And that's the question I have to ask both you and myself. Where else can we go? We have to "look to Jesus" because we have no other option. Jesus was no quitter, and I can't be a quitter either. Neither can you. We can stand our ground and refuse to quit because God hasn't and won't quit or give up on us.

Because people you love are watching you: "And ye shall teach them [to] your children, speaking of them when thou sittest in thine house, and when thou walkest by the way, when thou liest down, and when thou risest up" (Deuteronomy 11:19).

Dr. Wally Beebe, "Mr. Bus," who led me to Christ, loved me like his own sister and prayed for me faithfully every day until the day he went home to be with the Lord. He was more than a pastor and an evangelist to me. He was a teacher, a counselor, a brother, and a dear and precious friend. And he was someone who refused to let me quit.

I went through many struggles during the years of our friendship, and there were many times when I wanted to give up. But Brother Beebe challenged me every time by telling me there were too many people watching me for me to quit. His exact (and sometimes exasperating) words each time we talked about the latest crisis were, "Who will your kids learn from if not from you? You have to be the last apple on the tree! Don't you *dare* quit!"

Moses said something similar when he was telling the Israelites how serious they were to be about obeying the Lord. He said he wasn't speaking to the children because they hadn't seen God do the miracles or experienced His "greatness, his mighty hand, and his stretched out arm" the way their parents had (Deuteronomy 11:2).

Like the Israelite parents, I need to lay up those words "in my heart and soul" and live them each and every day. In doing so, I'm teaching the people I love how to do it as well. They may not be willing to listen to my words, but they can't help but see my walk. And the time is going to come when they will remember whether or not I was faithful in the hard times.

While it's my responsibility to teach them what I believe when they are young, it's also my responsibility to live what I believe even after they're grown. I must continue living out my faith when I'm "walking, when I lie down, and when I rise up." My kids will learn more from what I do than they will ever learn from what I say.

A precious friend of mine, who lives in another state, had to adopt her grandchildren to keep them from going into the system and being adopted by someone else. She called me one day and said, "Will you tell me again why I'm doing this?" She wasn't serious, of course, because she knows our choices are sometimes limited. But isn't that a great question?

As we talked about it, my friend and I agreed we can't make our kids or grandkids live for the Lord or choose to do the right thing. We hope they will, of course, but that isn't really why we're doing it. We keep on keeping on so our kids and perhaps our grandkids have our example when they reach a point of decision—so they have a choice.

Although we won't be able to make their decisions for them, we can make the right decisions ourselves. And we can do more than talk the talk; we can also walk the walk. You and I can't quit because the people we love are watching to see whether we are faithful.

Because God is sovereign: "Nay but, O man, who art thou that repliest against God? Shall the thing formed say to him that formed [it], Why hast thou made me thus?" (Romans 9:20).

In April 2011, Alabama was devastated by the largest single tornado outbreak in recorded history. There were 348 confirmed deaths as a result of those storms and nearly 11 billion dollars in damage. Just when we thought it couldn't get worse, another tornado hit. More than a year later, people in Alabama still had not recovered, and many were still asking, "Why?"

"Why?" is the question Job was asking, and if anyone had a reason to complain or to question God, he would be the one. He had lost everything: his wealth, his property, his kids and his health. He didn't even have the support of his wife, and his self-righteous friends were no help. Those "friends" assumed Job had done some terrible thing to bring the troubles on himself.

In the midst of these terrible tragedies, Job wanted to know why, and he said in Job 31:35, "behold, my desire is, that the Almighty would answer me," Well, Job got his wish. However, he should have been careful what he asked for because God's answer wasn't what he expected.

God didn't appear to Job from a burning bush or from a high mountain, but from a whirlwind, in the midst of a storm.

Rather than answering Job's question, God said, "Gird up now thy loins like a man; for I will demand of thee, and answer thou me." And then God asked some questions of His own. "Where wast thou when I laid the foundations of the earth?" (Job 38:3-4) and "Shall he that contendeth with the Almighty instruct him? he that reproveth God, let him answer it" (Job 40:2).

You see, Job began to think God was either unfair or had made a mistake because of all the terrible things that were happening. But all those terrible things were part of God's plan for this man even though Job didn't understand. God has a wonderful plan for my life too and for my prodigal. And He had that plan before He created the universe and laid the foundations of the earth. Where was I when God did those things? Where were you? Who are we to contend with or confront God as though we can instruct Him? And how do we dare to reprimand or rebuke God?

My friends Ronnie and Sandra Cheatwood lost their only son in a car accident caused by a drunk driver. Such devastation in their lives cannot be explained, and it began with a knock on the door in the middle of the night. Both parents struggled with trying to understand why their son, whose life goal was to be a medical missionary, had been taken from them. Ronnie wrote about their terrible loss in his book, *The Storm in the Middle of the Night*.[6]

Sandra told me what she learned more than any other thing is that God is sovereign. She learned He is not some indulgent grandfather or Santa Claus, but rather the omnipotent, omniscient God of the universe, who does what He does for His own reasons and without consulting us.

She came to realize it wasn't her place (nor is it ours) to question why God chooses to do things in a certain way. Job came to the same conclusion. When faced with those questions from his Creator, Job's answer had to be, "I am vile; what shall I answer thee? I will lay mine hand upon my mouth" (Job 40:4).

So another reason we can't quit is because we aren't the ones in charge. It's not our decision to make. We aren't always going to understand when heartaches come into our lives, and we don't need to. What we have to do is keep on doing the next right thing, do what we can do, surrender what we can't, and let God be God. Your life and mine will be much less complicated if we can remember we aren't the ones running the show.

Because there's a battle to be won: "when Daniel knew that the writing was signed, he went into his house…and prayed, and gave thanks before his God, as he did aforetime" (Daniel 6:9-10).

I've been listing the reasons we can't quit, and I've covered several reasons, good reasons, why we can't. But perhaps the single most important reason I keep going forward is I'm just too stubborn to quit. Now, I like to refer to myself as "single minded" or "tenacious." If asked, however, Harry and my kids would shake their heads and say, "Nope. She's just stubborn." And being stubborn isn't necessarily a bad thing.

Daniel 6 tells the story of how King Darius issued a decree saying anyone who prayed or asked a petition of God or any man other than the king would die by being cast into the lions' den. When Daniel heard the decree was signed, he went to his home and, with the windows open, he prayed just as he always had.

Daniel knew the consequences were going to be a lions' den and several hungry lions. Keep in mind he didn't know the end of the story like we do, but he prayed anyway. He could have done it quietly and secretly, but he refused to hide his faith in our great God. All the decree with its threat of death did was to make him more determined.

Some time back, I was devastated by what was happening in my kids' lives. I felt discouraged and defeated from the past, fearful in the present and hopeless about the future. Then I got mad. And I determined in my heart to have a stubborn, rebellious, defiant kind of faith, the kind that would enable me to say, "Though he slay me, yet will I trust in him: but I will maintain mine own ways before him" (Job 13:15). I had quit on the Lord once, and I was stubbornly determined it wouldn't happen again.

That determination led to my starting the "Joyful Noise Fellowship," which met for more than two years at my house once a month for singing and fellowship. I told myself and others Satan might be having a jolly old time in my family for 29 days out of the month, and I might shed tears on many of those days. However, on one day each month, there would be singing, rejoicing, and praising the Lord—not anyway, but because.

I thought God would make our monthly fellowship a blessing to me, and He did. But He also made it a blessing to others through me. Two of the men who were faithful to come every month became very ill soon after we stopped meeting and ultimately passed away.

Those two years were the last opportunity these precious Christian men had to use their voices to sing and to both encourage and be encouraged. And it could not...would not have happened if I had thrown up my hands and quit. When I refused to quit, it had an effect on my own life, but it also had an unforeseen effect on the lives of others.

Those of us who love a prodigal have a difficult path to walk, and we are sometimes subject to what I call "brat attacks." But if I'm going to pitch a hissy fit and bang my sippy cup on my high chair, I'm going to do it by exercising my stubborn will in refusing to quit. What about you? Can you get your spiritual back up and refuse to quit? If you can and if you will, it may just be that God will bless you and bless others through you.

Because the story isn't finished yet: "I was found of them that sought me not; I was made manifest unto them that asked not after me" (Romans 10:20).

If any of my readers are from Alabama, I may lose you at this point because I have to tell you I don't care very much about football. My daughter and my husband both love football—or I should say Alabama football—enough to make up for my shameful deficit. Although they would not miss one minute of an Alabama game regardless of who is playing against them, I don't often watch the games with them. I made an exception when Alabama played LSU on November 3, 2012. I'm glad I did because God taught me an important spiritual truth during the last two minutes of that game.

LSU was ahead 17-14 with less than two minutes remaining when they tried for a field goal, which should have ended the game. But they missed. The ball was then turned over to the Crimson Tide on their own 28 with a little more than a minute and a half left in the game. Alabama made three perfect passes and scored a touchdown with only seconds remaining in the game.

How did they turn it around? The answer is simple. They refused to quit. They were exhausted and battered and discouraged. And they looked it. One sports announcer said, "Even their legs look tired." But Alabama adamantly, emphatically, and unequivocally refused to quit. And I'm glad they didn't quit, because their story wasn't finished yet.

We can't quit either. No matter how hard the fight, no matter how powerful the opposition, no matter whether we are so exhausted "even our legs look tired." We can't quit. Our story isn't finished yet, and neither is the story of our prodigals. And it doesn't matter whether our prodigals have turned against everything we ever taught them about our God. God isn't finished with them, with me, or with you.

I know as well as you do our prodigals aren't seeking God. But they don't have to seek God because God is seeking them (Romans 10:20, Luke 19:10). It's not our job to point out what our prodigals "need to do" or to "fix" them. It's God's job, not ours, to reach them and to change them. Our job is to stand firm, refuse to quit, love and pray for them and continue to believe God. You and I can choose faith over fear and say with the psalmist, "for I shall yet praise him, who is the health of my countenance, and my God" (Psalm 42:11).

We can't quit even if it is the last minute and a half before the miracle happens. No matter how long we've been fighting or how exhausted and discouraged we are, the end of our story may be determined in the last few seconds. This truth, perhaps more than any other, is why we can't quit.

One final thought about how we can "keep on keeping on" in the midst of some awful circumstances is we don't have to do it forever. Only for today. I've given you some valid reasons why you can't quit, and God can give both you and me the strength to walk the path He has for us just for today. And because His mercies are "new every morning" (Lamentations 3:22-23), He will give us the strength we need for tomorrow. God hears our prayers, and the answer is coming in His time if we just don't quit.

Something to Think About:

What are some reasons you might be tempted to quit? What are some reasons you can't?

Part Five

Me Forgive Him? You Must Be Kidding!

"And be ye kind one to another, tenderhearted, forgiving one another, even as God for Christ's sake hath forgiven you" (Ephesians 4:32).

Forgiveness. It's a wonderful concept, isn't it? However, like all concepts, it's easier to talk about in the abstract than it is to apply in our everyday life. Still, I know God expects—more than that, God specifically tells me to forgive those who have hurt me, even when the wounds are deep and the pain is great. And forgiving someone who has hurt me deeply isn't an easy thing to do. If you love a prodigal, you sometimes wrestle with the same internal conflict, so you'll understand why I have struggled to find a starting place on the topic of forgiveness.

People much wiser than I have written about forgiveness, and the number of books available on the topic is staggering. However, forgiving as it applies to the continuous pain of loving a prodigal takes it to a whole new level, doesn't it?

You'd think it would be easier to forgive the people closest to us, those we love the most. But often it's more difficult to forgive them because the more we love someone, the greater the pain they can cause us. Those of us who love a prodigal have usually been hurt and disappointed so many times that forgiving the one who caused the pain can be difficult if not impossible.

Loving a prodigal can give us a lot of practice in the art of forgiving, so you would think, as often as we get to do it, we'd be better at it. But the reality is we're much more likely to add each new hurt to the list we've been keeping for as long as our prodigal has been acting out. And make no mistake about it. We *do* have a list, don't we? At least I do.

How is real, complete forgiveness going to happen? Our prodigals have ripped our hearts out, and, indifferent to our pain, have stomped on them with combat boots! Worst of all, they don't seem to care how much they've hurt us. How can I forgive those things? How can you?

Before we even begin looking at the ins and outs of forgiving, we need to start with this foundation: God doesn't "suggest" we forgive. While it's not one of the Ten Commandments, it *is* a directive. As with any directive, we have a choice of whether or not to obey. The hurt or offense and even the person who hurt us are only one part of the equation. Our willingness to obey God in the matter of forgiveness is the other. Whether I like it or not, and I often do not, they are separate issues.

I still sometimes struggle with seeing and accepting I don't have any power over the actions of the person who hurt me. I wish I did, but I don't. I do, however, have the power of choice, both in my response and in my willingness to forgive. The issue isn't about how we feel. It's about whether we are willing to obey God in the matter of forgiveness.

I've tried to find a way around Matthew 6:15, which says God's forgiving my trespasses is dependent on my forgiving those who trespass against me, but I can't find anything in the Scriptures to dispute this truth. And if forgiving people who hurt me is really a requirement for God to forgive me, it might be a good idea to take another look at forgiveness.

What does it really mean to forgive? Does it mean I need to forget what they did, to act as though the offense never happened? What about the terrible hurt, and what about the person who hurt me? Don't they have some responsibility too? And aren't some things unforgivable?

The best way to answer those questions is to look at some people who have forgiven the unforgivable. As we look at their pain and the choices they made about forgiveness, it may shed some light not only on what God expects from us, but also how powerful it can be in our own lives when we choose to forgive. After we've looked at their stories and what they learned, we'll look at how we can apply those truths in our own lives.

Resentment

Resentment is a sentiment
that I can ill afford.
So I just have to turn it loose
and give it to the Lord.

To pray for one who brought me pain
is more than I can do
in my own strength and power.
And yet I know it's true
that when I nurse resentment,
it hurts me much more than you.

By holding on to bitterness,
I buy into the lie
that I can drink the poison brew
and wait for you to die.

Chapter 12
A Whole Community Forgave the Unforgivable

Autumn is a beautiful time of year in Pennsylvania, and early October may be the loveliest of all. The leaves haven't reached their peak yet, but the trees still have plenty of color for people to enjoy. Pumpkin patches are everywhere, and the air is rich with the smell of apples and other fruits.

Lancaster County is mainly agricultural, so farms are common, and fresh fruit and vegetables are easy to find. Much of the harvest is in, and there's a dream-like quality to those brief days between the hard work of summer farming and harvesting and the winter, which is on its way. For one community at about 10:00 a.m. on Monday, October 2, 2006, the dream became a nightmare.

That's the day Charles Carl Roberts walked into the West Nickel Mines School, an Amish one-room schoolhouse, with a gun. He ordered the boys to help him carry some things from his truck into the classroom. Then he allowed the 15 boys, a pregnant woman and three parents with babies to leave, and he immediately barricaded the door.

He had kept the ten girls, ranging in age from 6 to 13, inside with him and told them to line up against the chalkboard. And shortly after 11:00 that morning, he began systematically shooting them, firing at least 13 rounds from his pistol.[7] Before it was over, five children had died, five were seriously wounded, and the gunman had killed himself.

Imagine the horror of such an ordeal and the intensity of what those poor parents must have been feeling. Such a brutal, violent crime committed against children is an outrage! That it happened to the gentle Amish people, whose faith requires they not resist such a cruel, violent crime, somehow makes it even worse.

When King Darius was forced by his own decree to put Daniel in the den of lions, Daniel didn't resist either. Early the next morning, after Daniel had been in the lions' den all night, the King went to the lions' den and "cried with a lamentable voice...O Daniel, servant of the living God, is thy God, whom thou servest continually, able to deliver thee from the lions?" (Daniel 6:20).

God was able to deliver Daniel, and He did. He was also able to deliver those Amish children. Yet, he did not. How can a parent, even a Christian parent, not ask why? How could someone—anyone—not want to seek revenge or at least justice?

How such a tragedy must have tested everything the Amish parents believed about themselves, their religion, their non-resistance, and even their God! What would they think and say, and how would they continue to serve the Lord? Hardest of all, perhaps, is how would they react to this crime against their children?

The only thing more amazing than the evil actions of Charles Roberts was the response of the entire Amish community. The fathers and grandfathers, leaders of their community, reminded the younger people that the murderer now stood before God, who would be his judge. And they admonished and reminded their people it wasn't their place to be his judge.

They also reminded their suffering community that Roberts had a wife and children and parents, who were also suffering. And then those broken-hearted parents did something I can't understand or even imagine.

People from the Amish community visited the Charles Roberts family and extended forgiveness to the killer's wife and parents. One Amish man held Roberts' father in his arms as he wept.[8] They even took food to the family of the man who had killed their children.

Why would they do those things for the family of someone who had brought such pain to them? It wasn't because they didn't love their kids. They did. Amish communities value their family relationships more than anything else in their lives except their relationship with God. How could they have forgiven the murderer and extended forgiveness to his family? How could we do such a thing?

The short answer is we can't forgive when we've been terribly injured. At least we can't forgive based on how we feel. Some things are so egregious, so terrible, so heart-rending, it would be and will be impossible for us to forgive. Sadly, not all of those awful things will come from strangers with a gun. They sometimes come from and through the people we love, people who should love us too.

The Amish church members are a community of people who value and cherish the simple things in life. They both love and live out a quiet country life, hard work, humility and their Christian faith. The depth of their faith and trust in the living God makes me look at my own, often weak faith, and it humbles me.

We won't know the depth and strength of our faith until it's put to the ultimate test. And if this wasn't the ultimate test, what do you think could be? It's bigger than anything I've ever had to endure. Those people had the kind of faith that makes it possible to do the impossible, to forgive the unforgivable.

What I learned from the Amish community's response is faith isn't believing God will answer our prayers in the way we want Him to. Nor is it trusting Him to put a hedge of protection around our loved ones, although there's nothing wrong with hoping and praying for either of those things. True, life-changing faith like theirs is trusting God when it seems like He hasn't answered our prayers, like He hasn't protected our loved ones. It's trusting Him when everything within us is screaming, "This can't possibly be Your will!"

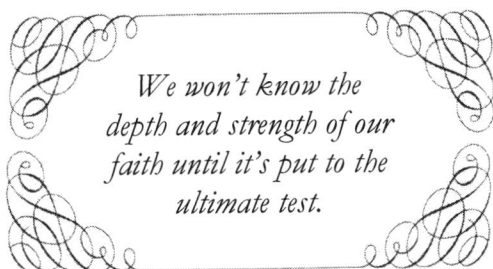

> *We won't know the depth and strength of our faith until it's put to the ultimate test.*

Some things in this world defy explanation, so how can we hope to understand them? Faith is choosing to obey God even when we don't understand the reason for our circumstances or our suffering. It's looking to God and trusting Him even and especially when we don't understand how someone could hurt us or hurt those we love.

Those devastated parents had to make the choice to forgive regardless of how they were feeling. And I'm certain those Amish families were not feeling any warm fuzzies about Charles Carl Roberts or his family. They made a decision to obey the Lord in the matter of forgiveness as a conscious action of their will. And they did it in spite of their feelings.

They knew and applied a truth I'm still struggling to learn and put into practice: that grief as terrible as this, by itself, is too heavy a burden to carry without the Lord's help. If we choose to add bitterness and unforgiveness to our load, it will crush us.

The West Nickel Mines School was torn down after the tragedy, and a new school was built near the original site. The name of the replacement school? The "New Hope School." It's a fitting name because in making the choice to forgive, they opened the door to healing, to joy, and to hope. It's what can happen when an entire community chooses to forgive the unforgivable.

Something to Think About:

Why do you think the West Nickel Mines Amish community forgave Charles Carl Roberts?

Chapter 13
Robert Smith Forgave the Unforgivable

Dr. Robert Smith Jr. is the Chair of Divinity and a Professor of Christian Preaching at Beeson Divinity School in Birmingham, Alabama. He has been part of their faculty since 1997, and he is one of the most respected and influential voices in Christian preaching in America today. He is also a broken-hearted parent and someone God has called on to forgive the unforgivable. This is his story.[9]

On the night of October 30, 2010, Dr. Smith and his wife Wanda were in Baton Rouge at the Bible on the Bayou Conference when they received a late-night phone call from their son Marcus. It was the kind of phone call no parent should ever have to receive—a phone call that would change their lives forever.

Their son Tony was living with and helping with the care of his grandmother in Cincinnati. He also worked at Richie's Fast Food Restaurant, where he was a cook. On that terrible October night, some men attempted to rob Richie's, and, when Tony was unable to open the cash register, one of the men shot and killed him.

Dr. Smith said before he knew his son was declared dead at the scene, he "turned [his] face to the wall like Hezekiah and begged God to spare [his] son's life." But God's answers are not always the ones we would choose, and a second phone call confirmed his son had died.

As Dr. Smith talked about his son, his voice sometimes quavered, and both his pain and his love for Tony were evident in his voice and in everything he said. He said Tony was a gentle man, who would literally "take the shirt off his back for someone else." Dr. Smith called it a "blessed flaw."

Kind-hearted and with many friends, Tony was a hard worker, who enjoyed serving and helping older people. In fact, Tony's primary reason for being in Cincinnati was to help his grandmother. He also loved the Lord, and the last time Dr. Smith saw his son, Tony had his Bible with him. Dr. Smith always knew God had a plan for Tony's life, and he fully expected God would call Tony to preach since "preaching was all over that boy."

But preaching was not God's plan for Tony's life, and everything changed on what Dr. Smith calls "that unforgettable day." What goes through a parent's mind when something so terrible happens—something so unexpected, so horrible, so unexplainable? Although he didn't address his feelings directly, the shadow of sorrow in Dr. Smith's eyes spoke more eloquently than any words could have.

Can you imagine the thoughts and the broken heart of Dr. Smith as he sat through the brief trial of the 17-year-old boy who took his son's life? Dr. Smith only saw the side of the boy's face as the sentence was read. Then he saw the front of his face only once when the boy turned and looked at his own mother. What he saw was a young man lost to society, at least for a while, and probably for a long while. Of course, his own son was lost to him forever on earth. But he also saw another parent whose heart was broken and realized not just one, but two mothers had lost their sons that day.

The young man who killed Tony didn't show any repentance or try to contact Dr. or Mrs. Smith. He didn't look at or speak to them. He never made an appeal to the judge or asked for forgiveness at sentencing or apologized in any way. What motivated Robert Smith to seek this young man out, to pursue and woo him until the young man would listen and then to give him complete and unconditional forgiveness?

Dr. Smith's hands trembled as he placed his palms together and held his fingers to his lips. Then he started to talk in a quiet but determined voice about the God he loved. He said God had begun to do a work of compassion and forgiveness in his heart. This broken-hearted father didn't talk about hatred or justice or revenge. In fact, Dr. Smith wrote his son's killer and told him God had changed his own heart to a heart of love for him. He also told this man, whom he had reason to hate, that God had a plan and a purpose for his young life. How could he do that?

As a hurting parent, Robert Smith didn't feel forgiving toward the young man who killed his son. Even as he talked about it, tears glistened in his eyes, and his voice was so low that his words were barely discernable. If true forgiveness was going to happen, God would have to do it. And He did. Dr. Smith didn't ask for any part of this journey, and there must have been times when he questioned how losing his son could possibly be God's will.

But as a father, a man, a child of the living God, Dr. Smith has found God faithful to work the loss of his son for his good and God's glory. He's found he can preach with greater credibility when he knows it's something God is doing in and through him. He's also found there is great power— God's power—in telling hurting people about forgiveness when he's willing to obey God himself by choosing to forgive.

Dr. Smith said it's not heroic on his part. It isn't even something he is doing. It's a work God is doing, and he is only cooperating with God by doing the action part of the work. He said, "Forgiveness is self-serving. Unforgiveness is too heavy to carry. Bitterness is too heavy to carry. Forgiving is more important for me than it is for the man who killed my son. Refusing to forgive him would eat me up."

In his soft, gentle voice, almost a whisper, Dr. Smith continued, "playing the video tapes of unforgiveness again and again will become perpetually obsessive until I'm consumed by it. If I let it consume me, I'll be missing all the wonderful things going on in my life. And I know I'll find those wonderful things if I only look for them."

Dr. Smith has learned a lot about himself through his personal tragedy, and he has a new understanding of the precedent God had set for him. He said, "God knows what it's like to lose a precious Son. God knows about our pain. He knows it intimately, and He understands it because He has experienced what I have experienced and more through His own Son." What Robert Smith has learned is best expressed in his own words:

"Losing my son made me a part of the 'community of fractured fellowship.' Being part of this 'fractured fellowship' has helped me understand how God uses pain redemptively. That is, He doesn't waste it, but He uses it to accomplish His purpose, for His glory and for my good. And if God doesn't waste our pain, neither should we."

"My family will never be the same. You don't 'get over' something like this," he said. "You only get through it. Forgiving the person who did it doesn't mean it's ok. It only means Robert Smith isn't going to carry it. I can't. It's just too big for me."

He's learned through his suffering just how insufficient he is. A false sense of strength, the "I can conquer anything" mentality, didn't work. How could it? How could he or anyone conquer or overcome such a terrible thing? Dr. Smith has stopped trusting in or drawing from his own strength and started drawing from a strength, a power beyond his own.

As our conversation was coming to a close, Dr. Smith turned to me and said, "You have put your finger on the pulsing heartbeat of my stimulus—my impetus. I've preached a lot about forgiveness in 48 years, and it's always been convenient, easy. Not this. Nothing like this."

He said God had spoken to his heart and said, "So you believe in forgiveness? What about this young man? Can you forgive him? And if you can't, how can you ever preach again about forgiveness to others?"

Like the Amish community in West Nickel Mines, Dr. Smith knew if his faith was real, so must be his forgiveness, whether

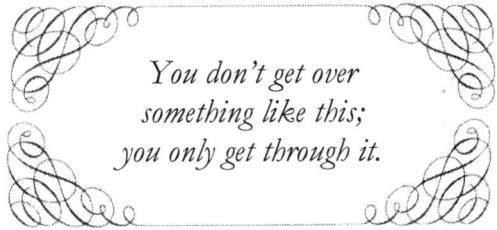

You don't get over something like this; you only get through it.

the offender sought his forgiveness or not. It was never about a communication between the killer and Robert Smith. It was about whether God's child was willing to trust Him and to obey Him by forgiving "even as God for Christ's sake had forgiven him" (Ephesians 4:32).

But Dr. Smith didn't stop with token forgiveness or forgiveness in word only. When he chose to forgive the man who killed his son and began to pray for him, he also made a decision to "put feet on his prayers." Through a long, complicated process, he began to communicate with his son's killer by letter. Keep in mind the man who killed Dr. Smith's son still hadn't asked for forgiveness. He hadn't sought out the family he had devastated, had in no way expressed regret.

In the beginning, his son's killer was suspicious about Dr. Smith's motive in writing him. In fact, he asked in one of his own letters how he could know Dr. Smith wasn't setting him up to be harmed or killed. However, Dr. Smith continued to pray and reach out through his letters, and the doors of communication continued to widen. The next step in the process, according to this amazing Christian man, is a visit at the prison with his son's murderer.

Why would Dr. Smith seek out this man, who had killed his son and who didn't indicate he was sorry he had done it? His answer was simple and to the point when he said, "None of us were looking for the Lord or for His forgiveness on our own. Left to ourselves, we never would have sought God. Instead, God sent His Son, who came to 'seek and to save that which was lost' (Luke 19:10) and to reconcile us to Himself" (Colossians 1:20-21).

Dr. Smith's story isn't finished yet. In choosing to obey God by forgiving his son's killer, he has opened doors, doors which never would have opened otherwise. And who knows what God might yet do in the life of that young man or in the life of a father who forgave the unforgivable?

Something to Think About:

Is it necessary for a person to apologize before we forgive them? Why or why not?

Chapter 14
God Forgave the Unforgivable

If you're a Christian, you already know the concept of forgiveness goes all the way back to Golgotha's hill and a wooden cross. That's where Jesus paid the price for our sins so we could be forgiven and reconciled to God. It wasn't because of anything we had done because, before redemption, we were the enemies of God (Colossians 1:20-21).

If I got what I deserved, if you got what you deserved, it wouldn't be forgiveness and reconciliation. But God is in the seeking, saving, redeeming and reconciling business. And I don't need to talk about that in the abstract because I've experienced it in my own life.

My husband was in Vietnam, and I was living in Florida with my three little kids. Although I had been raised Catholic, I was not a practicing Catholic. In fact, I wasn't a practicing anything. When someone knocked on my door in the summer of 1969, I didn't know it was the beginning of something that would change my life forever.

A preacher named Wally Beebe was at the door asking me to let my kids ride the bus to church. I was reluctant, but he was persuasive, and I agreed to let him pick the kids up the next morning.

Several things were happening in my life during that time; the most serious was four hospital stays among my three children over just four weeks. The last time, my youngest child, still a baby, was critically ill. I finally lost my job because I was busy with sick kids, and I didn't have the money to pay my bills. To say my life was upside down is an understatement. I knew the meaning of carrying heavy burdens when I wasn't much more than a child myself.

Not having a job freed me up to visit First Baptist of Ruskin with the kids, who had fallen in love with the church and the people there. The first Sunday I sat in the back pew and was out the door as soon as the preacher closed in prayer. But I had listened carefully to the preaching, and I went home with many things to think about.

> *I heard and believed God could forgive me and change my life. When I asked Him to do that, He did.*

A few weeks later, when Bro. Beebe preached on being born again. I saw myself and a lifetime of choices clearly for the first time. I won't minimize the burdens I was carrying on my young shoulders. Those burdens were staggering, and I was overwhelmed by them.

But I realized during an old-fashioned altar call that the burden I couldn't carry anymore wasn't my husband being gone, losing my job, or my kids being sick. It was the burden of my own sin, and as soon as the invitation was given, I went forward to receive Christ as my personal Savior.

I wasn't a sinner because of any specific sin in my life or even a whole series of them. The problem went much deeper, and I realized I was broken inside, separated from God, lost and alone. And it was because of my own choices. I heard and believed God could forgive me and change my life. When I asked Him to do that, He did.

On the authority of the Word of God, I can tell you my sins, like the woman Jesus talked about in Luke 7:47, were many, and God has forgiven me. But it wasn't because I deserved forgiveness. It was all grace then, and it continues to be all grace now because, no matter how hard I try, I can't and won't ever live a perfect life. Neither will you.

Please don't hear me promoting any particular denomination. Dr. James Dobson (Focus on the Family) is a Nazarene, Billy Sunday was a Presbyterian, Billy Graham is a Baptist, and C.S. Lewis belonged to the Church of England. A church "label" isn't what I'm talking about. What those men experienced individually at some point in their lives is what I saw that Sunday morning: that I was, at the core of my being, a sinner, who needed to be forgiven.

I've never gotten over the fact that God loved me enough to send His own Son to live the perfect, sinless life I could never have lived and then to die on the cross to pay for my sins. Nor have I ever gotten over the fact that Jesus loved me enough to willingly die for me, the just for the unjust.

Have you ever thought how our sinning against a holy God who loves us must have grieved His heart? He loved me in spite of the pain I caused Him, and He forgave me even though I didn't deserve it. Nor do I deserve it now. I owed a debt I could never pay, and God forgave my debt. Because He forgave me, God requires me to forgive the people who have hurt me—even when they don't deserve it.

But how many times are we supposed to forgive our prodigal and the others who have hurt us? In Matthew 18:21-22, Peter asked Jesus that very question. Peter thought he was being generous by asking Jesus if he was to forgive someone seven times because Jewish tradition only required him to forgive someone three times. However, Jesus said seven times wasn't enough, and Peter had to forgive seventy times seven. In other words, there isn't a limit on the times we need to forgive someone. It's every time.

A friend recently told me God doesn't forgive us unless we ask for forgiveness. My friend thought it logically followed that we don't need to forgive someone who has hurt us until the person asks for forgiveness. The problem with my confused friend's logic is we aren't God's peers. We are His creation, and we are totally accountable to Him.

He is the God who spoke, and the worlds and stars and galaxies came into being, who breathed the breath of life into man. He is the God who loved me and continues to love me, who paid the price for my sins, who forgave me and redeemed me and made me His own. He forgave the unforgivable. And He's the One who says you and I must forgive.

Something to Think About:

Has there been a time in your life when you needed and received God's forgiveness? Why should that cause you to forgive others?

Chapter 15
But You Don't Know My Awful Family!

"And be ye kind one to another, tenderhearted, forgiving one another, even as God for Christ's sake hath forgiven you" (Ephesians 4:32).

I have sometimes been so wounded, shattered, and outraged, I didn't feel like I could even begin to forgive the people who had hurt me. What about those times, and what about those people who hurt me? Don't they own part of it?

How I wish I could say they own it all! However, the hurt or offense and the person who hurt me are only one part of the issue. My willingness to obey God in the matter of forgiveness is another. Whether I like it or not, and I often do not, they are separate issues.

We almost never have any control over the actions of the person who hurts us. We do, however, have the power of choice both in our response and in our willingness to forgive. Does it mean we need to forgive and forget, to act as though the offense never happened? To answer that, we'll begin by looking at what forgiveness is not.

Forgiving a person does not mean we continue tolerating inappropriate behavior or abuse of any kind. The apology you get after your spouse has physically abused you or your children doesn't mean you have to stay where you and your kids are in danger and let that abuse continue.

A friend recently told me her prodigal had threatened her with a gun. She managed to take the gun, and then she called the police. Don't rush past what you just read. My friend's prodigal intended to kill her. After my friend called the police and the prodigal was arrested, she learned threatening someone with a gun is a felony. So she immediately began to question her decision to call the police.

You get the point here, right? She called the police because her prodigal tried to kill her and then she had second thoughts. What a perfect example of how the insanity infects every person in the home when a prodigal is acting out! Forgiveness does not mean we allow someone's behavior to endanger us or the children we are responsible to protect.

Forgiveness also doesn't mean we continue to enable our prodigals by bailing them out of trouble or we fail to hold them accountable. If the child support isn't being paid, forgiveness doesn't mean you let it go. If your prodigal has stolen your car, broken into your house, or forged a check on your account, he or she should be held accountable.

My own frustration is often not so much about forgiveness as it is about longing to have the relationship back. Perhaps yours is too. However, you and I can't make a relationship happen by ourselves. It takes only one healthy person to forgive, but it takes two healthy people to have a healthy relationship. Really forgiving from our heart doesn't necessarily mean we will have a relationship with our prodigals. Sometimes the healthiest thing we can do for our prodigal and for ourselves is to put some distance between the two of us...at least for a time.

But is it really forgiveness if we can't or don't spend time with our prodigal? Of course it is. If spending time with someone is required in order to forgive, how could we forgive people who have passed away? Having said that, I hasten to add that if we are ever going to have any hope of a restored relationship, it's going to include forgiveness. Your forgiveness. My forgiveness. In his book, *Just Like Jesus*, Max Lucado says, "Relationships don't thrive because the guilty are punished but because the innocent are merciful."[10] And he's right. You see, forgiveness isn't about our prodigals at all. It's about us and our choices. It's about our obedience. Now that we've looked at what forgiveness is not, let's look at what it is.

Forgiveness is an action. Ephesians 4:32 doesn't just tell me it's something I have to do, but it also tells me why. The reason I must forgive is because God has forgiven me. And He didn't forgive me because I deserved it or because of my own merit, but because of the merit of Christ. He forgave me for Christ's sake.

Micah 6:8 takes it even further by telling me God requires just three things of me, and one of them is to "love mercy." The phrase, "loving mercy," doesn't mean I just give lip service to forgiveness. It implies tolerance, acceptance, *Forgiveness means I give up my right to hurt you for hurting me.* and patience to go along with my forgiveness. Ouch! Not one of those things is high on my list of assets, especially when I'm hurt or angry. So it's a good thing forgiveness doesn't depend on my feelings.

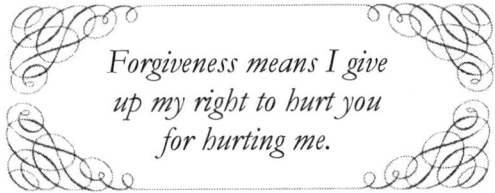

Forgiveness means I give up my right to hurt you for hurting me. It means someone has done something to me, created a debt of some kind. You might say, "They owe me!" Forgiveness means I officially and formally give up my right to exact payment of the debt. And just so I'm perfectly clear, giving up the right to strike back and collect the debt means I can't go back and collect it later. The debt is dissolved.

During the three years Harry and I had custody of our two grandkids, the parents did not pay a nickel of child support for the first year. Then they only paid it sporadically after they were court ordered to do so. Finally, Child Support Recovery had to enforce the order and collect the support.

They were also court ordered to reimburse us for medical expenses. However, when the kids were transitioned back to the parents, their parents still owed us about $3,000 in unpaid medical expenses. After the kids had been home for about a year, the parents sent a letter to us through our lawyer asking us to allow them to pay a small amount each month until they had paid it all.

I walked around in the yard, still brokenhearted over the whole situation, and praying God would give my husband and me direction. When I walked into the house, I asked Harry if he really wanted to do this for two or three more years, and he answered, "I don't want to do this for two or three more minutes." After praying together and talking it through, we composed a letter officially forgiving the debt. We had the letter notarized, and we mailed the original to the parents and a copy to our lawyer. By officially and permanently forgiving the debt, and doing it in writing, we knew we could never change our minds and collect it later. Legally, they were totally and completely off the hook.

I remember riding with Harry to the post office. But more than the drive, I remember the intense relief I felt when the drop box door closed on the mailbox. It was done. It was completed. It was finished, and I felt like the world had been lifted off my shoulders. My spirit was lighter than it had been for years.

You see, we didn't do it for the parents. And, as much as we loved those children, we didn't do it for them either. There was a debtor's prison, for sure, but we were the ones in the cell. We were as much imprisoned by the situation as they were by the debt. By letting it go, by forgiving the debt, we didn't just free them. We freed ourselves as well.

Those parents weren't repentant. Neither one had apologized for anything they had said or done. Nor have they apologized to this day. But you see, forgiving our prodigal isn't dependent on his or her being repentant. You mean I have to forgive him when he's not even sorry for what he did? That's exactly what I mean.

We don't forgive people because of what they say or do or what they don't. We forgive them because "God for Christ's sake has forgiven [us]" (Ephesians 4:32). My pastor calls it "grace for grace." And "grace for grace" doesn't mean forgiving him or her through gritted teeth. The same verse in Ephesians tells us we are to be tenderhearted and kind. As with the command to forgive, showing mercy and being kind are also a matter of our free will.

When we choose to forgive, we are also choosing to let go of the anger and hurt instead of harboring resentment. Or are we? My tendency is to nurse a hurt until it becomes a "root of bitterness springing up" in me (Hebrews 12:15). Maybe it's your tendency as well. However, that verse in Hebrews warns us the root of bitterness won't trouble the prodigal. It will trouble us. And if you love a prodigal, you have enough things to "trouble" you without adding to them.

Forgiving the debt wasn't about giving up our right to expect and require responsible behavior from people. It wasn't about "letting them off the hook" or not holding them accountable. In fact, it wasn't about them at all. It was about wanting to be free from the burden of our own anger and lack of forgiveness.

I'm not saying you need to forgive the financial debt. It wasn't about the money for us, and it almost certainly isn't for you either. It's about our broken heart. It's about our broken relationship. It's about the resentment you and I have been carrying for five days or 25 years. That's the thing we need to forgive. That's the thing we need to let go. The challenge for us is to separate the action and the person who hurt us from our responsibility to forgive and let it go.

Our prodigals aren't the only people we'll need to forgive as we walk this hard path. Before we've been walking very long, we'll have a whole list of people we need to forgive. It may include other family members, the spouse who set a bad example, our extended family who hasn't supported us through it. We might also need to forgive "friends" who have separated themselves from us like we have a contagious disease, the youth pastor who harshly criticized our family, and the pastor who assumed the worst of all of us. And we will also need to forgive ourselves.

Ourselves? Yes. One thing I know for sure is when we aren't forgiving others who have hurt or disappointed us, we aren't forgiving ourselves either. So our own names need to be added to the list of people we need to forgive. I've found when I start forgiving others, I'm better able to forgive myself. And when I'm compassionate about my own failings, it makes me better able to be compassionate about the failings of others.

So, no, I don't "know your awful family." But I do know mine. I also know that, regardless of how awful we think they are, the only way you and I will have any serenity or peace is if we're willing to forgive them. And isn't peace what your heart really longs for? It's available for those of us who are willing to obey the Lord by choosing to forgive.

Something to Think About:
Who are the people you need to forgive besides your prodigal? Is forgiving yourself on the list?

PART SIX

These Came Home

"And he arose, and came to his father"
(Luke 15:20).

Having your loved one act out in destructive ways may be a new experience for you. If it is, you may be totally bewildered. On the other hand, like me, you may have been walking this path for what seems like an eternity. Some of you have been praying with a broken heart for so long, you're discouraged. You may even have begun to ask yourself if there's any hope of your prodigal coming home.

You don't have to read very much of my book before you realize it isn't going to tell you how to "fix" your prodigal. In fact, it isn't going to tell you much about your prodigal at all. The purpose of *So You Love a Prodigal* is to help you learn how to take care of yourself when your family and your life are all upside down and crazy. It's also about finding the joy, which is God's gift to you, regardless of whether you have a prodigal in your life or not.

More than either of those, however, it's about reassuring you that God doesn't make mistakes. His will is going to be accomplished in the lives of your prodigal and mine, whether through their obedience or through their disobedience. But I don't want you to think there is no hope of our prodigals coming home.

Of course, we can have hope. And our hope doesn't depend on our prodigals seeking God because we both know they aren't seeking Him. However, they don't need to seek

God because God is looking for them. And He delights in seeking the lost and bringing back those who have wandered away (Ezekiel 34:16).

Every time a prodigal comes home to the relief and joy of his parents, it gives hope to the rest of us. The chapters in this section are going to tell you about some prodigals who did come home. As you read their stories, my prayer is you will be encouraged to keep on praying, to keep on hoping, to keep on putting one foot in front of the other until your own prodigal comes home.

In choosing the prodigals I was going to write about, I tried to combine a variety of life circumstances and to include all kinds of parents: absent parents, indifferent parents, ungodly parents, and parents who loved and served the Lord all their lives. I've also included a variety of prodigals, from those who only went a little way into the "far country" to those whose friends and relatives had given up hope.

I talked to many prodigals as I was researching and writing this book, and I found one common theme among all of them who had come home. The common thread was that God put someone in their lives, someone who was willing to love them where they were spiritually. That person also prayed for them consistently until the prodigal figured it out and came home.

As you read the stories of these prodigals who came home, I hope you'll see prodigals show up in all kinds of families and in all kinds of circumstances. I hope you'll also see no parenting "mistakes" are bigger than God. My prayer is you will in some way identify with and find hope in their stories.

God is still in the saving, redeeming, and transforming business, and He is no respecter of persons. What He did for them, He can do for us and for our prodigals. My story isn't finished yet. Your story isn't finished yet. Most important of all, our prodigals' stories aren't finished yet.

I can't stress enough how important it is for you and me to continue steadfast in prayer and find hope in trusting and believing our God knows what He's doing. He hears your every whispered prayer, and He sees your falling tears, my suffering friend. His answer will come, but it will be in His way and in His time. Not yours and not mine.

Homecoming

He's coming home; he'll soon be at the door.
Anticipation—Oh, the taste is sweet!
That I can kiss this child of mine once more,
Whose love for life this world could not defeat.
Nor could this wicked world keep him away.
He went away a child, returns a man,
Complex and hopeful, living day by day.
He's grown in spirit; I must too. I can
But live one single life and that my own,
And I can learn the balance—love, let go.
I too can strive to grow as he has grown.
And I can practice what I've come to know:
    That I can love him much, and it's all right,
    And I can hold him close, but not too tight.

Chapter 16
Billy Sunday Came Home

Billy Sunday was born in Ames, Iowa, to William and Mary Jane Sunday in 1862. Five weeks after Billy's birth, his dad, who was fighting in the Civil War, died of pneumonia. His death left Mary Jane widowed and with three small children. But losing his father so soon after Billy's birth was only the beginning of troubles for this baby, whose childhood consisted of one loss after another. Those losses included the deaths of his three-year-old sister and the grandmother he adored. However, his greatest loss happened when he was ten years old.

In 1872, Billy's mother was so poor she could no longer feed her children. So she made what must have been the most difficult decision of her life. She sent Billy and his older brother Ed to the Soldier's Orphan Home. How giving up her sons must have broken Mary Jane's heart! I can almost see her weeping as she put her boys on a train to send them away.

Those tragic losses had a profound impact on Billy Sunday. For the rest of his life, he struggled with losses and fear of abandonment. It doesn't sound like the kind of story that should have a happy ending, does it? How could a person, who started out this way, hope to turn out well?

Those four years in the Soldier's Orphan Home made a good and lasting impression on Billy. The Superintendent of the home, Mr. Pierce, was kind to Billy and taught him many things. And Mrs. Pierce read all the children Bible stories and prayed both for and with them.

Billy played baseball in the 1880s for the Chicago White Stockings (Sox). Baseball players didn't have a good reputation back then, and every bit of their "bad press" was earned. With all the losses in his life, Billy was a "ticking time bomb." His life wasn't yet one of extreme decadence, but he drank, he gambled, and overall was just a lost soul. He either forgot or ignored the early influence of his mother and the godly example and teaching of Mrs. Pierce. Although his life wasn't shipwrecked yet, he was well on his way to the "far country."

One day Billy was out drinking with his team in Chicago on an off day during the 1886 baseball season. As they were walking along, Billy stopped to listen to a gospel preaching group from the Pacific Garden Mission. But it wasn't the preaching that attracted him. It was the gospel hymns they were singing. He had first heard them at his mother's knee.

Can you imagine sending your children away like Billy's mother was forced to do? I can't, but I've never been in her position, so I also can't imagine having no food to give my babies. It's tough enough, but at least possible, for our generation of women to make a living as a single mom with little kids. For Billy's mother, it was impossible.

Billy's mother didn't have a lot to offer him in the way of spiritual training during the few years he lived with her. The only seeds she planted were the gospel songs Billy used to hear her sing. However, those few seeds brought forth fruit by attracting Billy to the group of people who were going to tell him about the Lord. God began to work in his heart that day, and he started attending services at the Pacific Garden Mission. The night Billy trusted Christ, it was a woman who put her arm around him and led him to Christ.

It both astounds and humbles me ho·
most feeble efforts. Billy's childhood r
ones—were very few. In fact, the
autobiography say, "I never saw my father.

Imagine the sad little boy Billy must have
perhaps always was. Can you see how one sweet memoɪ,
his mother's singing would touch his heart? His mom didn't
have a lot to offer her kids. She couldn't even keep them at
home. But while they were with her, she sang those hymns as
she cooked or cleaned or sewed. It wasn't much of a seed,
was it? But God used that tiny seed to change Billy's life.

Billy Sunday went on to become one of the most
influential evangelists of the early 20th century, and he
remained faithful throughout his life. He didn't stumble or
quit when his own sons became prodigals, when his oldest
son committed suicide, or even when his only daughter died.
Billy stayed faithful until his death in 1935.

How important was the little bit Mary Jane Sunday had to
offer? Well, someone you might never have heard of was
saved at one of Billy Sunday's revivals. His name was
Mordecai Ham. Mordecai Ham went on to preach the gospel
as well, although he never achieved fame like Billy. However,
at one of his services, a man named Billy Graham came
forward and gave his life to Christ. What do I need to add to
that? And it started with a mother, who didn't have anything
to offer except the gospel songs she sang to her kids.

Billy came home.

Something to Think About:

If a parent doesn't have much to offer, do you think God can
use the little bit they do have? Why or why not?

Chapter 17
Mel Trotter Came Home

Mel Trotter's story is more than just the story of a prodigal who came home. It's also the story of his mother, Emily Jane, who never stopped praying for him and never gave up on him or on her God. If ever a mother had reason to despair over her circumstances, Mel's mother did. And Emily faced those circumstances alone because her husband was an unsaved alcoholic, who owned a bar. It's also the story of Mel's broken-hearted Christian wife and how God can "restore the years that the locusts have devoured" (Joel 2:25).

Mel was born in 1870, and I'm sure his mother had dreams for him just as we did for our kids. However, Mel Trotter was a rebel from his youth. Although his dad would have paid for him to go to school, Mel had other ideas and dropped out. By the time he was 16, he was working as a barber and earning a "man's pay."[12]

Like our own prodigals who are acting out, having money wasn't necessarily a good thing for him. Mel started gambling and drinking heavily. By the time he married Lottie Foster four years later, he was already an alcoholic whose life was out of control. And why would he not become an alcoholic when his father and both his brothers were alcoholics? If you and I need an example of how substance abuse affects an entire family, we don't need to look further than the Trotter family.

Mel tried several things to control or stop his drinking, but none of them worked for long. He moved from the city to the country thinking it would help him stop. Of course, it did not. And just like our prodigals have promised us they would stop acting out, Mel promised his wife again and again he was "finished" only to be drunk again by the next night.

He finally stopped going home when he was on a binge, and he would be gone four or five days at one time. I can picture his poor wife watching the door and jumping at every sound, wondering if it was Mel coming home or the police to tell her they had found his body. I wish I could say we don't know how she must have felt, but we know those feelings all too well, don't we?

However, Mel Trotter reached a new low even for the worst prodigal I've ever heard of. After a ten-day drunk, he staggered home to find his two-year-old son dead in his wife Lottie's arms. Surely this would be the final straw, and Mel would do what was right and stop breaking the hearts of the people who loved him. In fact, he promised his wife over the body of their dead baby that he would never touch another drop of alcohol.[13] Did he keep his promise?

You already know the answer, don't you? Within two hours after the funeral for his little son, Mel was drunk again. Even as I'm writing this, my heart aches for his sad, desperate wife, for his entire family, and for all the rest of us who love a prodigal. How could she hold on to hope? How can we?

But can't you feel just a little compassion for how Mel Trotter was suffering? Because he was. Mel blamed himself for his baby's death, and how could he not? Where was he when his wife needed him? When his son needed him? However, his son's death wasn't going to make him stop drinking. That's not how the disease of addiction or alcoholism works. In fact, the anguish and guilt only caused him to drink more, to stay away longer, to sink lower until he had abandoned his wife and was homeless.

Without a job, a family or friends, Mel had finally reached bottom. He was drunk and had been thrown out of a Chicago bar in January, 1897, barefoot because he had traded his shoes for one last drink. He planned to commit suicide by throwing himself into Lake Michigan. Why not? He couldn't imagine living without alcohol, and he couldn't imagine any way to continue living with it. He couldn't face his life the way it was anymore, afraid to live and afraid to die. He hated himself and his life and had determined to end it.

But what about his mother's faithful prayers, which continued even though she saw her son sinking deeper and deeper in sin? What about the prayers of Mel's faithful wife, who never stopped praying for him and doing the right thing herself? What about them? And what about us? God heard their prayers, and He hears ours. He saw their tears, and He sees ours. Like my prodigal and yours, Mel wasn't looking for God. But God was looking for him.

It didn't matter what Mel intended. God had other intentions, and He was bigger than Mel's plan, bigger than his failures, bigger than his despair. As Mel was staggering past the Pacific Garden Mission, he heard people singing, "Throw Out the Lifeline Across the Dark Wave," and he paused. That was all it took for someone to pull him inside the warm building and sit him down.

Before the night was over, Mel heard the gospel and received Christ as his Savior. And in the moment when he prayed, "God be merciful to me, a sinner," he remembered all the times he had heard the story of Christ and the cross of Calvary. He was the epitome of the prodigal come home.

Your prodigal may not have gone as far into sin as Mel Trotter, or he may have gone even further. It doesn't matter how far our prodigals go when they run away from God and everything we hoped and dreamed for them. It doesn't even matter whether they are looking for God or seem to have totally lost their way. Like our prodigals, Mel Trotter appeared to be lost, but God knew where He was.

Mel Trotter came home.

Something to Think About:

Can a prodigal go so far there is no hope for him or her? Why or why not?

Chapter 18
Yvette Maher Came Home

When I first met Yvette Maher, I was delighted by her charm, her immediate welcome, her bubbling laugh, and her concern for others, which is so much a part of who she is.[14] Although the purpose of my visit was to hear her story, she managed at one point to change the topic to my prodigal, and she prayed for me and for my prodigal before I left.

But I also saw a shadow of pain in the eyes of this remarkable woman. And her pain drew me to her and created an immediate connection. What could have caused such a shadow in the eyes of the former Senior Vice President of "Focus on the Family?" I was about to find out.

Growing up on a farm in Kentucky makes for a simple life for families. Yvette's days were filled with hard work and simple pleasures. In the early days, Yvette's family even worshipped at the church where generations of their family had worshiped.

If alcohol, drugs, and infidelity were happening in her family, Yvette wasn't aware of it. She remembers laughter and affection being a regular part of their family home. They all hugged and kissed one another before they went to bed, and her family seemed like any other family. Their seemingly "normal" family interactions are what made it such a shock when she was 17. That's when Yvette's dad told her mom about his affair and said he wanted a divorce.

Yvette's mom sobbed and begged him to stay, and she continued to fall apart emotionally every time he visited the house. Although Yvette's mother was a Christian, she found herself in the middle of a major depressive episode. In fact, her mom was so devastated by the divorce, she had no emotional energy left over for her daughter.

So Yvette suffered not only her dad's physical abandonment but also her mother's emotional abandonment. And while Yvette was hurt and angry at her father for leaving, she was also disgusted with her mother for begging him to stay.

Yvette deplored her mother's dependence on her father. She wanted her mom to fight back or to be something more than a doormat. And as much as she loved her mother, she couldn't respect her. When Yvette needed her mom to "suit up and show up," her mom just wasn't able to do it. She was too consumed by her own grief and loss.

Please don't hear me condemning anyone who has been divorced. My first marriage ended in divorce too, although I tried my best to keep it from happening. So I understand our choices are sometimes limited, and divorce might be the only option. However, nobody "wins" in a bitter divorce, except the lawyers. And the kids, like Yvette, who deserve to have love and care from both their parents, often lose more than anyone else.

After the divorce, Yvette's dad would sometimes refuse to speak to or even acknowledge Yvette or her sisters when he would see them in a store. The ongoing rejection for no discernable cause made a deep wound and caused an emptiness in Yvette, both of which may last a lifetime.

The divorce and her father's rejection caused Yvette to feel conflicting emotions, despair one moment and rage the next. She both loved and hated her father, who had broken her heart, and her mother who spent her time weeping and begging him to stay.

A year after the divorce, Yvette and her mom lost the family home, and her mom was forced to live in a hotel room. Yvette wasn't willing to move into a hotel room, so she stored her few belongings in her car and tied a mattress on the roof.

Yvette slept at the homes of various friends, most often at her best friend Lona's house. Lona and her family were Christians, who loved the Lord. They also loved Yvette, but their unconditional love and influence didn't stop Yvette from acting out in some very destructive ways. Her acting out behavior reached a new level as alcohol, drugs and promiscuity became her way of life…anything to fill the emptiness inside her.

When Yvette was 19, she found out she was pregnant. Her boyfriend had no intention of marrying this girl from the wrong side of the tracks, so Yvette chose to have an abortion. Even after Yvette's abortion, Lona and Lona's parents continued to love her unconditionally and to treat her with the same kindness they always had.

It's been a long time since her abortion, but the pain in Yvette's voice as she told me about it was as wrenching as it must have been the day it happened. My heart ached for the tender-hearted, wounded girl she was back then—a girl who thought she didn't have any other choice but to do what she did.

If Yvette was out of control before, the abortion sent her to new lows. Tormented by what she had done, she began acting out in ways she'd never thought of before and doing anything she could to somehow lessen her pain and emptiness.

Like many prodigals, Yvette decided to try a "geographical fix" by moving to Colorado. Before long, she was involved with Tommy, and they moved in together. Several months later, she was pregnant again. Although she initially decided to have another abortion, she couldn't go through with it this time. Eventually, she and Tommy were married, and their twin girls were born a few months later.

About a year after Yvette and Tommy were married, and after the birth of their son, Yvette and Tommy relocated to Kentucky. Yvette didn't know it, but moving to Kentucky was about to change her life. She still drank, smoked marijuana and had a vocabulary like a sailor's parrot. But her new next door neighbor, Ranie, was a Christian.

Not only was Ranie a Christian, but she was also a praying Christian. Like Lona, she loved Yvette unconditionally and prayed for her. And she was about to reap a harvest from the seed Lona and her family had planted years before.

One weekend, Yvette went to her high school reunion, intending to party the entire time. However, God had other plans. On the first night, she saw the emptiness of the group and her own emptiness. Disgusted with all of it, she knew she wanted more than what her life had been and still was.

She felt dirty, and, when she compared her life with Ranie's life, she wanted to be clean like her friend. She was sick of her life, sick of the emptiness, sick of the bleakness of her own soul, and she longed for forgiveness.

Early the next morning, Yvette was in the car, weeping, broken and headed home. As she was driving home, with tears streaming down her face, Yvette prayed the most unorthodox "sinner's prayer" I've ever heard. She said, "I will give You a year and trade my crap-life for what You have for me."[15]

What brought it about? Lona and Lona's family had planted the seed, Yvette's mom continued for years to pray for her, and Yvette's friend, Ranie, had been up all night praying for her too. God hears our prayers, and He heard theirs, and a prodigal started home.

Yvette's decline was a process and so was her homecoming. That alcohol-drinking, pot smoking, foul-mouthed woman didn't turn into the Senior Vice President of "Focus on the Family" overnight. It was a process, and it took days and weeks and months and years of spiritual growth and the influence of Christian friends. Those first Christian friends loved her until she could become someone who could love herself.

Those years Yvette spent in the "far country" left some wounds that will never heal completely. Her eyes were sad as she said, "Being a prodigal who comes home doesn't mean we don't have consequences. I still grieve the choices I made back then, especially the promiscuity. I know I'm forgiven, but, like David, 'My sin is ever before me'" (Psalm 51:3).

Yvette came home.

Something to Think About:

Do you think her parents' divorce was partly to blame for Yvette's acting out? Why or why not?

Chapter 19
Douglas Roark Came Home

When I met with Douglas Roark in the touring bus for The Old Paths, a gospel quartet, I had already heard parts of his story. Now I was anxious to hear his whole story from the beginning and in his own words.[16]

He smiled when I said, "You give me hope personally," and his first words were, "My mother never gave up on me." This hopeful theme carried throughout his entire story, and I was both challenged and comforted as he told me that story.

Douglas's mother was a faithful, radiant Christian, who did her best to introduce Douglas to Christ and to raise him to live a godly life. He grew up in church and knew all about Jesus, but he didn't *know* Jesus personally. He didn't have any anger or hostility toward the Lord or toward religion. He just wasn't interested.

Douglas's dad was a low-bottom alcoholic, who lived on the railroad tracks and in boarding houses for most of his life. Although Mr. Roark finally trusted Christ at a place called "A House of Prayer" later in his life, he was never a part of his kids' lives. Growing up without a father left a terrible void in Douglas's life, and that void may have been one of the reasons Douglas went down the path he did. But it was also the very thing God used to reach this lost and desperate young man.

Douglas smoked his first joint when he was nine years old. He said it didn't seem like a big decision to get high the first time. But it wasn't very long before he began to smoke marijuana regularly and to hang out with others who drank, smoked, and used drugs.

If alcohol or drugs are part of the problem with your prodigal, you already know alcohol and drug use are progressive. Douglas wasn't an exception, and he was only 14 when he stuck a needle in his arm for the first time. From then on, this lost teenager, hardly more than a baby, lived to "shoot up" and learned how to survive in the streets.

Douglas was arrested when he was 17 and was placed in a treatment center in a 12-step program. But he didn't stay there very long because he didn't want sobriety any more than he wanted to know the Lord. He left the treatment center, and, running from the law, ended up in Monroe, Georgia. He felt sure a new location would help him get a new start and he would be able to stop doing the "heavy drugs" and use only marijuana and alcohol.

A geographical "fix" hasn't worked for others, and it didn't work for him either. He couldn't outrun his problems or "turn over a new leaf." How many times have our prodigals promised they would do the same thing? By the time Douglas was 20, he had a $300-$500 a day cocaine habit and was selling drugs to support his habit. The drugs drove him, and everything he did was dictated by this need.

"But God…" Don't you love those words? Here was this young man, hooked on drugs, about as far away from God as a prodigal could be and with no desire to become a Christian. He wasn't looking for God, but he had a mother who wouldn't give up. His broken-hearted mom continued to pray for him and refused to quit. And God heard those prayers.

When Douglas was 23, he went to work for a bi-vocational preacher named Joe Hicks. Joe was a big-hearted, godly man, who would often begin his sentences with the word "Son" when he was talking to Douglas. Douglas said about Joe Hicks, "He had no idea of the power of that one word to a boy who never had a dad."

For four months, Joe built a relationship with this long-haired hippy with the sunken cheeks and dead eyes until he really did become like a father to him. Then came the day they were having "Friend Day" at Joe's church, and Joe asked Douglas to come and be his friend. Douglas agreed to go, not realizing it was the beginning of a great change in his life.

Douglas didn't trust Christ that day, but hearing the gospel created a restlessness in him, which lasted all week. He went back to Joe's church the following week on Father's Day, 1992, and when the invitation was given, he received Christ as his personal Savior. It took for Douglas what it's going to take for our prodigals: a divine intervention by a God who loves them even more than we do.

I asked Douglas what one thing was a constant through those years he spent "in the far country." His answer was immediate, "I had a mom who lived out Psalm 40:1, 'I waited patiently on the Lord, and He inclined unto me and heard my cry.' She refused to give up on me or on the God who could and finally did change my life."

I also asked Douglas what he would say to the person who is reading this now, the one who loves a prodigal, whose heart is broken and who is ready to give up. This was his answer:

"Don't give up. Continue to have faith and believe God can do something wonderful. Continue to be the one they can run to. You don't have to approve of or accept what they're doing to love and accept them. Let Christ in you be the 'Hope of Glory' and live for the Lord in front of them.

"Christ is in the life-changing business, and He is able to save your precious prodigal and to bring your prodigal back home. Stay faithful until He does."

Douglas came home.

Something to Think About:

Why is it important for you to stay faithful until your prodigal comes home?

Chapter 20
Rita Came Home

Say what? Where in the world did that come from? Weren't you the one who tried to hold it together when everything was falling apart? Weren't you the Christian school teacher, the soul winner, the one who was going to have a home different from and healthier than her family of origin?

Weren't you the one whose heart was broken over her husband and kids, who prayed for those kids and continues to pray for them? Yes, and yes, and yes. I was and did or at least tried to do all those things. But there's more to the story, of course. Isn't there always?

My kids weren't perfect. Indeed, they didn't need to be, and all of them had their own share of issues at one point or another as they were growing up. But our lives didn't get really crazy until we moved to Virginia. Within two years of the move, some of my kids began to act out in ways I never dreamed they would.

Their acting out started with the "wrong crowd" and skipping school and escalated to alcohol and drug use. Two of my kids ended up going to in-patient treatment, one of them multiple times. I struggled through sleepless nights full of worry and multiple days of the same. Instead of seeing the dreams I had for my kids fulfilled, I was facing the nightmare of loving a prodigal. Knowing their potential, I was stunned as I saw my hopes for them in ashes. Where I had once joyfully prayed for their success, I instead found myself frantically praying they would not die from the wrong choices they were making. Fear was my cruel and constant companion.

During the insanity of all those things, my husband told me about an affair he'd had, and—oh, by the way—he was leaving. Desperate, I warned him our marriage and our entire family were so fragile, neither could survive a separation. And I begged him to stay. However, he was adamant about what he was going to do. And he left.

It was the last straw, and I was finished, "finito," "fertig," done! I had loved and served the Lord for more than 25 years for this? No! It was too much! I had chosen God over the world, and I thought He would bless my family. How could He not when I wanted nothing more than to serve Him and have my kids do what was right? Now my husband and my kids had disappointed me, and I was devastated, broken and bitter. In my despair, I remembered every time I had been disappointed by pastors, churches or Christians. So there was plenty of resentment to go around.

I wasn't really angry at my husband, my kids, or my church, however. I was angry at my God. I had tried to raise godly kids, to be a godly wife to a man who didn't love the Lord the way I did. When my ex-husband left, it was the final straw. When he turned his back on me and on our family and walked away, I turned my back on God and walked away, too. I also stopped going to church. It wasn't a conscious decision—more a frame of mind. If I had chosen God over the world, and this was the result, then, like Peter went back to fishing, I would go back to "the world." And that's exactly what I did.

I started running with a group of other divorced and separated people, and I even began drinking alcohol. I worked all week, and I partied all weekend. You couldn't have convinced me God cared about me if you and I together had seen Him write it on the wall. And I must have been the most miserable human being who ever lived. During that time, I didn't bear any resemblance to a Christian much less to the Christ I had once asked to be my Savior.

If you had asked me back then why I was acting out, I would have answered, "If your kids broke your heart and your husband walked away when you needed him most, you'd act out too. If you felt judged and criticized unfairly by your family, your friends, and your church, you'd walk away too. And, most of all, if you had been betrayed and abandoned by your God, you'd give up too!"

Although I sometimes dated during those years, I wasn't looking for a relationship. I was as finished with men as I was with God. Then I met Harry, and, although I tried to run him off, he didn't run. I don't know what that humble, gentle man saw in me because I certainly wasn't a prize back then. I remember the first time he told me he loved me. I told him not to mention "love" to me again and added, "If you knew me, you wouldn't say you loved me." Besides, I no longer believed love existed except as a tool to manipulate people.

But Harry wouldn't give up, and, as he continued to be steadfast with his presence and his kindness, I began to love him and even to trust him, in spite of my fighting it every step of the way. Learning to love and trust Harry didn't mean I was willing to trust God, however. I had tried the way of walking with the Lord, and I wasn't willing to try it again.

The thing is, no matter how much I tried to run from God, I couldn't run far enough or fast enough. I may have felt lost but, just as with our prodigals, God knew exactly where I was. I may have given up on God, but God had not given up on me. I may have turned my back on God, but He didn't turn His back on me. I may have forgotten I had asked Him to be my Savior many years before, but He hadn't forgotten. I may have thought I was "finished" with God, but He was not finished with me. Not even close.

When Harry and I had been married a little more than a year, it became necessary for us to take custody of two of my grandkids. The older child was an eight-year-old girl, and the little guy was five. The parents were in trouble with drugs and were going to lose the kids for medical neglect. You see, the five-year-old had leukemia, and the parents' problems meant he wasn't getting the required treatment.

Harry and I had to take a "crash course" in the care of a child with leukemia, and it didn't make my heart tender toward my kids or toward my God. Instead, it fueled my anger. But the painful Neupogin shots I had to give that brave little guy and the many hospital stays with him began to melt the block of ice my heart had become. And trying to comfort that sick baby, who sucked his thumb and sometimes cried because he wanted his mother began to break down the protective walls I had built around my frozen heart.

Each time I tried to reassure his sister everything would be all right, I had to look in her little face and see her grief, her anger, her fear. All those things forced me to look at their pain and to realize I wasn't the only one hurting. Others were hurting too, and some of them were hurting more than I was.

Then there was our church. Although I felt the "social club" church Harry and I had been attending once in a while was good enough for us, I didn't think it was enough for the kids. However angry I was at God and however much I thought He didn't love me anymore, I was still sure He loved those children. So I began looking for a church that could minister to them. The church I found was Capital Baptist Church, pastored by Steve Reynolds.

One day Harry had to wait at the school for our granddaughter to get back from a field trip. When they were delayed, he looked for something to read, and all he could find in the car was my Bible on the back seat. He started to read it, but not in any particular place. He began to read the verses I had highlighted, the notes I had written in the margins, and the promises I had claimed years before. He saw the places where my tears had smeared the ink. And as he read, his gentle heart was broken both for the Lord and for the person I had been. This was a Rita he did not know.

When he came home, he asked me what all of it meant: the highlights, the notes, the tears, the promises. So I told him about the August 17 church service many years ago when I had received Christ and what had led up to my conversion. He didn't ask any questions, but only a few weeks later he went forward during the church service and trusted the Lord himself. With Harry's conversion, more of the walls around my angry heart began to fall. And underneath that anger, I found the pain.

I remember trying to pray, not understanding all the terrible things I had experienced or how God could have allowed them. Like yesterday, I can hear myself asking God, "What do You WANT from me?" Several weeks later, I was reading Rick Warren's book, *The Purpose Driven Life,* and the Holy Spirit touched my heart when I read the words, "God wants you to grow up!" I knew it was the answer to the question I had asked weeks before.

Talk about an epiphany or an "Aha" moment of seeing what should have been obvious all along! Who was I to tell God what to do in the lives of my kids or even in my own life? I remembered God's asking Job, "Where were you when I laid the foundations of the earth?" (Job 38:4), and I realized I had been acting like a spoiled, petulant child. Because things

169

didn't go the way I wanted them to go, the way I thought they should, I had decided to pitch a temper tantrum and walk away.

Healing and restoration began that day, but it wasn't a one shot deal. It has taken years to develop a new and close relationship with the Lord. Again and again, I've had to claim God's promise that He will never forsake me (Deuteronomy 31:6). I also have to keep reminding myself God has forgiven me (1 John 1:9), and I have days even now when I struggle with guilt and shame and doubt.

God has restored my fellowship with Him, and it's sweeter than it ever was. Today I can choose to respond rather than react when I don't like what's happening in my life. I don't do it perfectly, but I don't have to be perfect today and neither do the people I love. Turning my will and my life over to the care of God each day reminds me I'm not the one in charge, and I don't need to be.

However, the mistakes I made during those years, the sins I justified or just didn't care about are things I will never forget. The bitterness I nursed left me with scars and regrets, and they won't be completely healed until Christ returns. Like David, "my sin is ever before me" (Psalm 51:3). Like Adam and Eve, the fellowship has been restored, but the innocence is gone. And I did it to myself.

Rita came home.

Something to Think About:

When your heart is broken, what can you do to make sure you don't start acting out yourself?

A Final Word

I want to leave you with two thoughts. The first is that you and I can't control when our prodigals will come home or even whether they will. However, other prodigals have come home, and we can—we must—continue to pray for our prodigals until they too come home. Until they do, we can trust that God's purpose in our prodigal's life will be accomplished whether through their obedience or through their disobedience.

What we can count on in the meantime is that our God knows about our broken heart. He sees every tear we've cried, and He hears every desperate prayer. And He would not allow these terrible things to happen if He weren't going to use them for His glory and our good. It isn't an easy journey, but we can count on God's faithfulness to walk this hard path with us. We don't have to do it alone.

The second is that you don't need to "go to the far country" just because the people you love have broken your heart. Nor do you have to jump on the merry-go-round just because everyone else has done it. I've been to the "far country," and it isn't a nice place.

It isn't necessary for you to rebel against a God who really does know what He's doing. You don't have to walk away because you don't like what God is allowing in your life. The Christian out of fellowship with his or her God must be the most conflicted and unhappy of all creatures.

A final word for those of you who have walked away and have become a prodigal yourself: Come on home. God's "hand is not shortened, that it cannot save; neither his ear heavy, that it cannot hear" (Isaiah 59:1). If you can't hope in your God, where do you think you will find hope? Come home and bring your broken heart so you can let God's healing mercy restore you.

God is bigger than your pain, greater than your anger, and His love and forgiveness are more extravagant than you can imagine. Giving back to His control what you never could have controlled yourself will give you back your peace. Come on home.

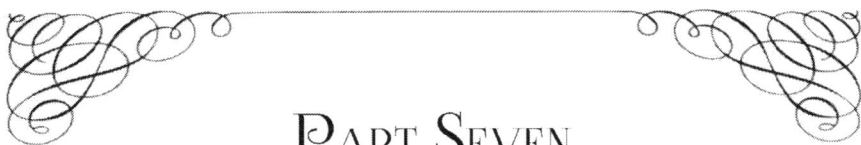

PART SEVEN

Bringing It All Together

> "Weeping may endure for a night, but joy cometh in the morning" (Psalm 30:5).

We've looked at prodigals and the people who love them from every perspective available. We've looked at who's to blame, and we've examined every detail of the parable of the prodigal son in Luke 15. We've looked at what we can and can't do and why we can't quit, and we've looked at prodigals for whom there seemed to be no hope. We've posed questions and tried to answer them, and we've even questioned God. Now we're coming to the end of this book, which I hope has been helpful to you.

However, we're still faced with two questions. The first of these is whether God can fix the mess our family is in. Can the God of the Bible really "go before me and make the crooked paths straight?" (Isaiah 45:2). The answer is He not only can, but He will. However, He will do it in His time and in His way rather than in our own. As we look together at the way God works to repair what's broken in our lives, my prayer is you will entrust your broken pieces to Him and wait for Him to create something beautiful with them.

The second question is how can we take care of ourselves until He does? How can we survive the insanity of loving a prodigal without falling apart—or worse—becoming a prodigal ourselves? Those of us who love a prodigal are sometimes our own worst enemies when it comes to setting ourselves up to fail. I've listed some of the ways we tend to "shoot ourselves in the foot" in this process of recovery as well as some ways we can avoid doing that. The suggestions came from hundreds of people, and I've found many of them helpful. I hope you will too.

Under His Feathers

I know a place of refuge
where I can run and hide
from storms that rage around me
and those that rage inside.
This place gives peace and comfort
from every painful thing:
Under His feathers, Under His wing.

He bids me come and rest there
to find a sweet surcease.
And there from all my burdens,
my weary soul finds peace.
I know I'll find acceptance;
there's nothing I must bring:
Under His feathers, Under His wing.

He draws me close beside Him,
and bids me peace, be still.
Then He gently teaches me
to trust His sovereign will.
Depending on His mercy,
it's to His cross I cling:
Under His feathers, Under His wing.

Oh, wonderful that haven,
that precious hiding place,
where I can flee from trouble
and seek my Savior's face;
where He dries every teardrop
and teaches me to sing:
Under His feathers, Under His wing.

Chapter 21
Can God Fix This Mess?

"And we know that all things work together for good to them that love God, to them who are the called according to his purpose" (Romans 8:28).

We can't, but God can: If I've emphasized one thing more than any other in this book, it would be that you and I can't "fix" anything or anyone. However, God can. Our job is to take our hands off and let Him do it in His time, in His way and according to His purpose.

No one will ever be able to explain to your satisfaction or my own why tragedy has entered our lives. And it *is* a tragedy when your husband walks out on you. It *is* a tragedy when you've raised your kids to live for the Lord, and they walk away from Him and from you. It *is* a tragedy when you bury someone you love.

Those who pat our hands in the middle of our storm, verbalize a few platitudes and then go back to their lives don't help; they only add to our pain. They almost never really comprehend our loss and our pain, all of which are real and sometimes overwhelming. How can we not sometimes ask, "Why?" "Why my kids, my husband, my health, my sorrow?"

Along with the Serenity Prayer, Romans 8:28 may be the words most memorized by people who have a broken heart. What a comfort it can be to know all things, even the terrible ones, will work together for our good. But there's more to it.

The original Greek text places the word God a lot closer to the beginning of the verse than do our English translations. Romans 8:28 would be better translated, "And we know *God causes* all things to work together for good." (Emphasis mine)

Had you asked me to define "synergy," I would have told you it meant the sum is greater than the combination of the parts. While that's true, it means much more. "Synergia" is a Greek word, meaning the *creation* of a

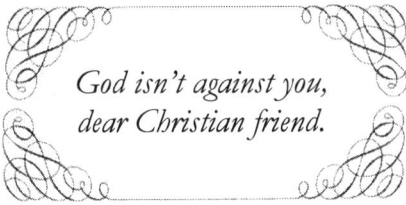

God isn't against you, dear Christian friend.

whole, which is greater than the parts. Bottom line: the result God is going to bring about would not come to be without all the parts, and I do mean *all* the parts. The "new" thing God is creating from this terrible time you're going through will be an entirely new and wonderful creation by our great Creator God.

God isn't against you, dear Christian friend. He is for you, He is for me, and He has allowed some things to come into our lives to bring about an end, which wouldn't and couldn't happen otherwise. He's an artist who recycles terrible things and makes them into something beautiful, something for our good.

Although I don't have all the answers, I can assure you God hasn't made any mistakes. When our spouse betrayed us or our daughter started using drugs, God didn't say, "Whoa! I never saw THAT coming!" None of those things surprised Him. In fact, nothing in my life or yours has ever taken Him by surprise.

You see, God doesn't come along like the Red Cross after the catastrophe happens. He's there before it begins. He's there in the beginning when our child is arrested or our husband walks away. He's there in the middle when we've lost our hair to chemotherapy or our child is in the hospital from an overdose. And He's there at the end when we may begin to see the plan He has been developing all along.

I don't understand today, and I may never understand why it takes a tragedy to work a miracle. But I know the difference my broken heart has made in my own life and in the lives of others. It was a gift, although it wasn't the gift I would have chosen. I wish I could sing like Sandi Patti or draw like Thomas Kinkaid or create an entire world like C.S. Lewis. However, those are not the gifts God gave me.

What God gave me instead was a broken heart and the ability to write about it in a way that brings people hope. My path hasn't been an easy one, and I know yours hasn't been any easier. We know about pain, don't we? But Dr. Smith was correct when he said, "God uses pain redemptively." All God needs from us is our willingness to let Him use it.

But what about my broken heart: God wants to use your broken heart too. And He will if you let Him because He delights in using broken vessels. I can best illustrate this truth by telling you about our grass—or rather, our lack of grass.

For the last two years, we've tried to get grass to grow in our back yard. Good grass. Lush grass. Any grass. I would have settled for crabgrass just to have something green back there. Then I heard some of the sod farms in our area will let people pick up the broken pieces from their fields after the sod has been cut. Cutting the sod results in some of the squares being broken, and nobody is willing to pay for broken sod. Those pieces are left where they fall or are kicked to the side like trash.

A sod farm flourishes not far from our house, and every time we drive past it, my eyes are drawn to those fields. I'd like to tell you I'm admiring the beauty of the grass, but that wouldn't be true. Sometimes I'm coveting those broken pieces and wondering how I can get some of them. At other times, I'm shaking my head at what a waste it is to leave them or throw them away.

One day as we were driving past, I saw a man with a truck and trailer. He was walking along the rows, gently picking up those broken pieces of sod. Then he was carefully putting them on his trailer. He treated each broken piece as if it were precious and valuable.

Left to themselves on the side of the sod field, those broken pieces would have died, their beauty never nurtured and developed. But the man I saw didn't leave them laying there. What others thought were worthless, he saw as having value. He gathered up the broken pieces of sod others had rejected and walked away from because he had a plan for them.

I didn't follow that man home, but I didn't need to. I knew what he was going to do. He was going to take those broken pieces of sod and make something wonderful from them. Those pieces weren't pretty or dear or precious to anyone else, but they were valuable to him. He didn't just see the broken pieces. He saw the beautiful thing they could become.

We can't see the beauty of what that man created with the broken pieces, but do we really need to? You and I can be certain he didn't go to all the trouble of picking up those pieces just to throw them away. He had a plan for them, and his plan didn't include wasting them or throwing them away. It also didn't include leaving them where they had been cast aside.

God isn't going to let our pain go to waste either, my hurting friend. If you and I will let Him, God will gather up the pieces of our broken heart. He will take every rejection, every accusation, every disappointment, and every tear. He will take the broken pieces of your heart—of my heart—into His gentle hands, and He will make something beautiful.

God is still on the throne, and He knows about your broken heart just as He knows about mine. Our story isn't finished yet, and God is going to make our ending better than our beginning (Job 8:7). Trust Him and take care of yourself until He does.

Something to Think About:

Do you think God is able to make something good come out of all the craziness of loving your prodigal?

Chapter 22
Bible Basics for Taking Care of Yourself

I've already covered some basics about how to take care of yourself until your prodigal comes home. So I won't repeat them here. However, I want to do more than just survive, don't you? I want to thrive! I want to have the joy God said is my "portion under the sun" (Ecclesiastes 9:9). And you and I don't have to wait until our prodigal comes home for that to happen. What are some things we can do to take care of ourselves so we will have that joy?

Stop comparing: "For where envying and strife is, there is confusion" (James 3:16). Envy isn't limited to material things, talent, position, or success, is it? Those of us who love a prodigal would trade any or all those things just to have our prodigal do what's right and to have our relationship restored. Broken relationships hurt, and there's nothing wrong with looking directly at our hurt sometimes and feeling sad.

However, it can become a problem when we look at the relationships others seem to have and compare them with our own. It's only a baby step from comparing to envy, and several problems come along with envy. The first problem is we seldom see others completely or clearly—the way they really are.

You and I can't know what a relationship is really like between two other people. We can only see their lives through the window they have opened to us. What we're actually comparing is our inside with their outside. Because of our limited vision, we can't make an accurate comparison. We also can't know God's plan for their lives or the burdens those people must carry on their path. We only know our own. No wonder James 3 says "envying causes confusion."

Comparing our path with the path of others is envy at its ugliest because it implies God has somehow treated us unfairly. And isn't that what envy is really about? Taking care of ourselves means you and I need to let go of any envy and stop comparing our circumstances with those of others.

Take a break: "And he said unto them, Come ye yourselves apart into a desert place, and rest a while" (Mark 6:31).

Jesus had sent His disciples out to begin preaching and healing. Now they had returned, and they were so surrounded by needy people, they didn't even have time to eat, much less to rest. Jesus told them to take some time apart to rest. It's what they needed, and we need it too.

You've no doubt heard the debate about whether a glass is half full or half empty. How you and I see the glass is supposed to determine whether we are a pessimist or an optimist. I don't know how accurate that little test is. However, I know for sure that if you stretch your arm out and hold a half-full (or half-empty) glass in front of you for a while, it begins to get heavy. And the longer you hold it out there, the heavier it gets. Eventually, it will be too heavy for you to hold any longer, and you'll have to lay it down.

Not too long back, I was devastated by some things going on in our family. I was so devastated, in fact, I couldn't even write for my blog. In addition, I had some medical issues, and my doctor told me I needed to resign as director of our church's "Heart to Home" Ministry.

Harry went with me to meet with our pastor when I tearfully resigned. Our pastor, who knew all the things we were facing, listened carefully. Then he told both of us it was past time for us to take a break. He suggested we take some mini-trips or even a long trip, anything that would get us away from the insanity of our family situation for a while. His exact words to Harry were, "She's been walking this hard path for too long without a break. Get her out of Dodge for a while."

Our pastor was right. I was so exhausted I had nothing left to give to a ministry, to my writing, to my family, or to my God. I needed to come apart and rest, and so do you. Loving a prodigal isn't an easy journey, and you may be doing this for a long time. Give yourself permission to take a break.

Dig a well: "Blessed is the man...who passing through the valley of Baca make it a well" (Psalm 84:5-6).

The valley of Baca can be any place of testing, wherever or whatever it may be. It's the barren, desert place, the wilderness of a broken heart. Those of us who love a prodigal know it only too well.

The first thing I notice about this verse is the word "through." You and I are passing *through* the valley of Baca. When we're suffering and filled with fear, it's hard to remember we won't be there forever. But our circumstances are temporary, and we don't have to carry that burden forever. We just have to carry it today.

Then there's the option of "making a well" while I'm there. Digging a well? Are you crazy? It's taking everything I have just to survive, and now you're telling me I need to dig a well? Can we really make a fertile place in this desert and in the wilderness of our broken heart? Yes, we can. However, when you love a prodigal, it might take some serious well digging in your valley of Baca.

No matter where our wilderness journey takes us, we can choose to make it a rich and vibrant garden rather than a barren place. I sometimes think digging a well has less to do with our spirituality and more to do with the right exercising of our will. A combination of good old-fashioned stubbornness and an unwillingness to quit sometimes digs a well.

The third thing I see is the one going through the valley of Baca is "blessed," and "blessed" means happy. Happy? How can we be happy when someone we love is struggling with addiction, has made bad choices, has shamed and humiliated us, and has wrecked his or her life? A better question is, "how can we not?" If you and I choose to waste all our time grieving and worrying

> *When we're suffering and filled with fear, it's hard to remember we won't be there forever.*

about the relationship, the person, the situation we don't have, we won't be able to rejoice in or enjoy the ones we do have.

Our prodigals and our pain about them are part of our lives, but they are not the whole. Nor should they be. Are you willing to spend your entire life grieving one person who broke your heart instead of enjoying the wonderful gift you have of a brand new day and the other people who love you? I'm not. It might mean changing my perspective, but I can choose to find joy in today whether my prodigal gets it together or not. And so can you.

Abraham Lincoln said, "Most people are about as happy as they make up their minds to be."[17] And he was right. I believe the key is changing my perspective, remembering my circumstances are temporary, and picking up my shovel.

Avoiding relapse: "I press toward the mark for the prize of the high calling of God in Christ Jesus" (Philippians 3:14).

Avoiding relapse is a real concern even after our prodigals have come home. That's especially true if alcohol or drug abuse is one of the problems your family is facing. However, the tendency to return to unhealthy or destructive behavior isn't limited to substance abuse alone or even to our prodigals. You and I are as likely as they are to return to unhealthy behavior. What does that look like?

The students in the court referral classes I teach have all been arrested for something related to alcohol and/or drugs. Most of them are there for a DUI. One of my students, a man in his 50s, told me his wife insists on smelling his breath every time he comes home from work. Smelling his breath? Really? At 50 plus years old? How crazy is that? And he isn't the one making her crazy. She's doing it to herself.

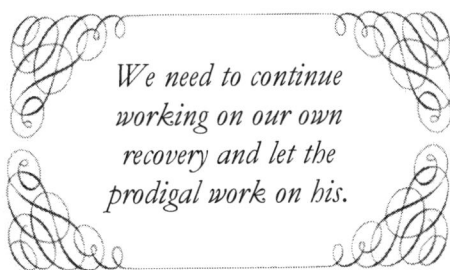

> *We need to continue working on our own recovery and let the prodigal work on his.*

Another (adult) student's mother somehow found my phone number and called me. She first asked me "how he was doing." Keep in mind my job requires absolute confidentiality, so I couldn't tell her anything even if I wanted to. Which I didn't, and I don't. Then she wanted to know where she could "make him go get help."

I understand fear is the underlying cause of both those behaviors. And I know what it's like to live in fear. So do you. But my answer to them was the same answer I have for you and for myself. There's a program for us, and it's not our prodigal's program or recovery. We need to continue working on our own recovery and let the prodigal work on his.

If you have tried some of the suggestions in this book and have applied some of the promises and principles, you've begun your own journey of recovery just as I have. And we need to be on guard so we don't revert back to our old behaviors and reactions. If they didn't work before, why would you think they might work now?

There's a calling on your life, dear Christian friend—you and I have been called to love a prodigal. I'm not going to tell you it's an easy calling. There's nothing "easy" about loving a prodigal. But it is a calling, nonetheless. And, like every calling of God, it's a high calling.

Our job—yours and mine—is to continue to press on, doing the best we can, learning from our mistakes and growing along the way. And grow we must! Because it was too miserable and overwhelming the way it used to be, wasn't it? The way we used to be. But as we learn to let go of the things we can't control and begin to work on ourselves, the growth will come.

However, a lifetime of trying to control people and situations beyond our control won't be changed or overcome in a week or a month or a year. And if we're not careful, we'll find ourselves checking their text messages "just this once" or calling their sponsor "just to find out how they're doing" or following them "just to be sure they went where they said."

We need to stop those things before they even begin. We need to recognize them for the unhealthy actions they are and refuse to give in to them. We need to plant both feet and determine in our hearts to go forward and continue to grow rather than turning back. It's one of the most important things we can do to take care of ourselves.

Expect A Miracle: "But he knoweth the way that I take: when he hath tried me, I shall come forth as gold" (Job 23:10).

I love butterflies, don't you? They're both beautiful and interesting. Butterflies spend most of their lives in the larval stage as a caterpillar close to or on their source of food. They crawl along willy-nilly and eating, eating, eating like a horde of Baptists at a fellowship dinner. Until one day, for seemingly no reason, they begin to build and develop a chrysalis, which will cover their little caterpillar bodies while an amazing transformation takes place.

Once the chrysalis is fully formed and surrounds the caterpillar, the caterpillar's body begins to break itself down into what's called "undifferentiated" cells, somewhat like stem cells. Scientists don't believe the caterpillar feels pain, and they may be right. However, the chrysalis itself is sensitive to touch, so I have to wonder whether the caterpillar does feel pain. I tend to think a process harsh enough to turn your body into "mush" isn't very comfortable.

You and I are going to change too. And here we are again, looking at ourselves instead of at our prodigal. But you see, our prodigal's life and journey aren't the only ones God is working in and through. Neither is our prodigal the only one God is going to change. Like the process in the caterpillar's chrysalis, our heartaches will change us, and great and repeated heartaches will change us greatly.

God isn't going to let those heartaches go to waste. He's using them to conform us into the image of His Son (Romans 8:29). Like me, you may have wondered if God has forgotten you and forgotten the people you love so much, if He's closed His ears to your prayers and your pain. But Job assures us God does indeed know "the way that [we] take." Job also knew when "God had tried him, he would come forth as gold" (Job 23:10). And so will we.

We can't see through the outer shell of the butterfly's chrysalis, but God can. What looks like total destruction and devastation on the inside is an opportunity for God to make something new and better. And it's what He does, both for the butterfly and for us. In some way scientists can't understand, those cells begin to form into something new and better in a process which defies logic and can only be called a miracle.

Do you need a miracle? Have you prayed for years, and it seems like God doesn't hear or care if your heart is breaking? I know it's the way I sometimes feel. And yet I really do know God can and will use my problems, my prodigal and even my pain to make something beautiful if I'll just let Him. What looks like total destruction to me and to others is the perfect opportunity for God to work. Maybe the miracle God is going to perform is the difference you will make in someone else's life by your example, your faithfulness, your obedience.

I don't know about you, but I like things to happen quickly, and I'm not usually patient with the process. However, most things, especially the wonderful ones, are just that—a process. If we broke the chrysalis open before God had finished the work He was doing, we wouldn't find a butterfly. But when the process is complete—when God has finished the work and performed the miracle in the butterfly's life or in our own lives, we'll find the result was worth the wait.

Something to Think About:

What can you do if you notice yourself slipping back into your old, unhealthy behaviors?

I hope you've been encouraged from reading my book and that you've found some reasons to "press on." More than anything else, I hope you will choose to trust our great God on your hard path and to believe He'll never make you walk it alone.

Resources

Disclaimer: These resources are provided only as a starting point for you to seek help. They are not intended to be a substitute for professional psychological, psychiatric or medical advice, diagnosis, treatment or legal advice. Always seek advice from your personal physician or qualified (licensed) health service provider and your own lawyer. While I'm glad to provide you with these resources, neither the groups listed nor I can guarantee results. The internet addresses and/or phone numbers were correct at the time of publication and may have changed.

- -

Your Regular Doctor/Practitioner: Your primary care and mental health practitioners can often provide referrals for substance abuse treatment or support groups for the family.

- -

Your Local Hospital's Chaplain: The chaplain at your local hospital can provide referrals to support groups. In addition, many hospital chaplains oversee support groups at the hospital and may provide individual counseling at little or no cost.

- -

Your Pastor or Priest: Many pastors and/or priests have training in counseling and can be a valuable resource for counseling or referral to local support groups.

- -

Your Attorney: Consult your attorney regarding any legal issues which may arise due to the actions of your prodigal.

- -

Adult Children of Alcoholics:
Internet: www.adultchildren.org
Telephone: 310–534–1815

- -

Alcoholics Anonymous (AA):
Internet: www.aa.org/lang/en/subpage.cfm?page=1
Facebook: facebook.com/groups/1590853867808538/
Telephone: 212–870–3400
See "Alcoholism" in your local phone directory.

- -

Al-Anon - Family Support Group for Families of Alcoholics:
Internet: www.al-anon.org

- -

Al-Anon Alateen - Teen Support Group for Families of Alcoholics:
Internet: www.al-anon.org/alateen-for-teens
Facebook: http://bit.ly/2fdX4x5
Telephone: 757–563–1600

- -

Al-Anon Alateen Meetings Nationwide Directory:
Internet: www.al-anon.alateen.org/local-meetings
Telephone: 888–425–2666

- -

Celebrate Recovery:
Internet: www.crgroups.info
Internet: www.locator.crgroups.info
Facebook: www.facebook.com/celebraterecovery

- -

Dual Recovery Anonymous (DRA):
    Internet: www.draonline.org
    Facebook: www.facebook.com/DualRecoveryAnonymous
    Telephone: 913–991–2703

- -

In the Rooms:
    Internet: www.meetings.intherooms.com
    Facebook: www.facebook.com/intherooms

- -

Learn About Alcoholism:
    Internet: www.learn-about-alcoholism.com

- -

Mothers Against Drunk Driving (MADD):
    Internet: www.madd.org
    Facebook: www.facebook.com/MADD.Official
    Telephone: 877–275–6233

- -

Narcotics Anonymous (NA):
    Internet: www.na.org
    Facebook: http://bit.ly/2eBc86J
    Telephone: 818–773–9999

- -

National Institute on Alcohol Abuse and Alcoholism:
    Internet: www.niaaa.nih.gov
    Telephone: 301–443–3860

- -

National Institute on Drug Abuse:
    Internet: www.nida.nih.gov
    Telephone: 301–443–1124

National Institute of Mental Health:
  Internet: www.nimh.nih.gov
  Telephone: 866–615–6464

National Clearinghouse for Alcohol and Drug Information:
  Internet: www.samhsa.gov
  Telephone: 800–729–6686

Opioid Treatment Program Online Directory:
  Internet: www.dpt2.samhsa.gov/treatment

Overcomers Outreach:
  Internet: www.overcomersoutreach.org
  Facebook: http://bit.ly/2ffMaao
  Telephone: 800–310–3001 /-or-/ 562–698–9000

Teen Challenge:
  Internet: www.teenchallenge.org
  Facebook: www.facebook.com/teenchallenge

Treatment Referral National Helpline:
  Internet: www.samhsa.gov/find-help/national-helpline
  Telephone: 800–662–4357

ACKNOWLEDGEMENTS

A book like this doesn't happen without the help and influence of many people. When one begins to list them, someone is sure to be forgotten. My apologies if you are that someone. Having said that, there are several people I need to thank:

Myra Binns Bridgeforth, who walked the beginning of this journey with me. David Sloan, who first made me believe this book should be written. Peggy Williams, who put aside her own pain to read what I wrote, telling me what worked and what didn't. Yvette Maher, Douglas Roark and Dr. Robert Smith, who so graciously shared their stories with me. Jennifer Rash, who consistently reminded me how important my book and Precious Prodigal Ministry are. Chris Tiegreen and David Bennett for seeing something of value in my words and publishing them. Shawnette Daniel for her proofreading and suggestions and for believing I can do anything. My Writers Anonymous regulars, who inspire me with their energy and their beautiful words. Sue Walker for baby-stepping me through this entire process with gentle nudges and suggestions, for her continued investment in words and the people who write them, and for investing in me. Ellen Sallas, for the beautiful formatting and cover design and for having the patience of Job with my edits. Harry for his web design, for reading every word I write, for encouraging me and so much more. And for teaching me to hope again.

Harry and Rita, 2016

To contact Rita for an event or to share what you've learned on your own journey of loving a prodigal, email her at: MyProdigal@RitaMoritz.com.

Discover More Online
    Internet: RitaMoritz.com/MyProdigal

For more information about Rita Moritz
or our Precious Prodigal Ministry, visit:
    Internet: RitaMoritz.com
    Facebook: fb.me/AuthorRitaMoritz

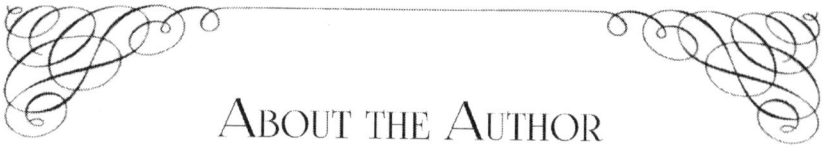

ABOUT THE AUTHOR

Rita Moritz is a writer, poet, blogger, editor and speaker. She has been published in *Educational Leadership, Indeed* Magazine, and *Open Windows*. Her poetry has been published in various publications and has won many awards. She has published one collection of poems, *Precious Poems: A Journey of Hope*. Her "Precious Prodigal" blog has about 25,000 hits each month.

She teaches in Alabama's Court Referral Program where she helps people change their destructive behavior and begin to make healthier choices. She is the founder and president of Writers Anonymous, a monthly writing group. Under her leadership, members of Writers Anonymous have brought home more than 75 awards. With the help of her group, she plans and coordinates the Mid-Winter Writers Conference each year. She and her husband Harry are co-editors of the *Muse Messenger*, the monthly newsletter of the Alabama State Poetry Society.

Whether writing her blog, leading her writing group, planning a conference or teaching, her upbeat approach to life is an encouragement to others. She knows what it's like to have a broken heart over a prodigal. And she knows how to find the wonder in each day...even in the days that aren't wonderful.

More Praise for *So You Love a Prodigal*

If you've felt the pain of loving a prodigal, you're very familiar with the ups and downs of the heart and the twists and turns of the mind in times of uncertainty. Rita is familiar with them too, and she has a lot to say about those unsettled thoughts and feelings in *So You Love a Prodigal*. Her compassionate and biblically centered insights will encourage and strengthen you. Even more, they will help you continue to love your prodigal—and your God—without giving up.

Chris Tiegreen, Author
Former Managing Editor, *Indeed* Magazine.

If you are someone who loves a prodigal, I highly recommend Rita Moritz's book, *So You Love a Prodigal*. In her book, Rita addresses the issue of loving a prodigal with wisdom and compassion and in a conversational tone that will encourage you and give you hope. This book will make a difference in your own life and possibly in the life of the prodigal you love.

~ Sue Brannan Walker, Author,
Publisher Negative Capability Press,
and former Alabama Poet Laureate, Mobile, AL

Also available from
Rita Aiken Moritz:

RITA AIKEN MORITZ

Precious Poems

A Journey of Hope

"Rita's work speaks of family and faith, of delight and despair, but with the hopeful cords of God's grace and goodness tying them together."

~ Joe Whitten, author of *Learning to Tell Time* and past President, Alabama State Poetry Society.

ENDNOTES

1 Rita Roberts (Now: Rita Aiken Moritz), "Toughlove for Kids at Risk," *Education Leadership Journal*, Alexandria, VA, Volume 51, Number 3, November 1993, 81-82, Online at: <http://www.ascd.org/publications/educational-leadership/nov93/vol51/num03/Toughlove-for-Kids-at-Risk.aspx>.

2 "Census Bureau Reports 64 Percent Increase in Number of Children Living with a Grandparent Over Last Two Decades," U.S. Census Bureau, Revised 19 May 2016, 8 Jun. 2016, <http://www.fatherhood.org/father-absence-statistics>.

3 C.S. Lewis, *The Problem of Pain*, San Francisco, CA: Harper, 2001, 91.

4 Kenneth Bailey, "Meaning of Prodigal Son Parable," 1 Apr. 2016, 7 Jun. 2016, <http://www.eprodigals.com/The-Prodigal-Son/The-Prodigal-Son-Motives.html>.

5 Kenneth Bailey, "Meaning of Prodigal Son Parable," 1 Apr. 2016, 7 Jun. 2016, <http://www.eprodigals.com/The-Prodigal-Son/The-Prodigal-Son-Motives.html>.

6 Ronnie Cheatwood, *The Storm in the Middle of the Night*, Morgan Hill, CA: Bookstand Publishing, 2011, 135.

7 David Kocieniewsli, "Man Shoots 11, Killing 5 Girls, in Amish School," *New York Times*, 3 Oct. 2006.

8 Joshua Hood, "What the Amish School Shooting Can Teach Us About Forgiveness," 15 Jun. 2012, 8 Jan. 2016, <http://joshuamhood.com/amish-forgiveness>.

[9] Dr. Robert Smith Jr. (Charles T. Carter Baptist Chair of Divinity and Professor of Christian Preaching, Beeson Divinity School in Birmingham, AL), interview by author, 8 Oct. 2014.

[10] Max Lucado, *Just Like Jesus*, Nashville, TN: Word Publishing, 1998, 22.

[11] Lyle W. Dorsett, *Billy Sunday and the Redemption of Urban America*, Grand Rapids, MI: William B. Eerdmans Publishing Co., 1991, 8.

[12] City Vision University, "Mel Trotter," 3 Feb. 2016, 4 Apr. 2016, <http://www.cityvision.edu/wiki/mel-trotter>.

[13] City Vision University, "Mel Trotter," 3 Feb. 2016, 4 Apr. 2016, <http://www.cityvision.edu/wiki/mel-trotter>.

[14] Yvette Maher (Executive Pastor at New Life Church, Colorado Springs, CO), interview by author, 17 Dec. 2012.

[15] Yvette Maher, *My Hair and God's Mercies…New Every Morning: A Story of a Life Changed by Grace*, Colorado Springs, CO: Focus on the Family, 2012, 42.

[16] Douglas Roark (Founder of The Old Paths), interview by author, 13 Nov. 2012.

[17] Abraham Lincoln, "Quotes of Abraham Lincoln," BrainyQuotes.com, 2016, 12 Jul. 2016, <http://www.brainyquote.com/quotes/authors/a/abraham_lincoln.html>.